WHAT NO ONE HAS TOLD YOU:

How Insiders *Really* Get Jobs

Signe A. Dayhoff, PhD

What No One Has Told You:
How Insiders *Really* Get Jobs
by Signe A. Dayhoff, PhD

Copyright © 2016 by Signe A. Dayhoff, PhD
Published by Effectiveness-Plus Publications LLC
80 Paseo de San Antonio
Placitas, New Mexico 87043-8735

Illustrations by Signe A. Dayhoff
Cover design by around86 at fiverr.com, Fotosearch.com

ISBN: 978-0-9970168-2-6

Disclaimer: This publication is designed to provide accurate and authoritative information in regard to the subject matter covered. It is sold with the understanding that the publisher is not engaged in rendering legal, financial, or other professional services. The instructions, ideas, and advice in the book are not intended as a substitute for counseling. The author and publisher disclaim any responsibility or liability resulting from application of procedures presented or discussed in this book.

DEDICATION

This book is dedicated to all job seekers who, through no fault of their own, have not been able to put their best foot forward to present and promote themselves to potential employers even though they have had the skills, abilities, expertise, and experience to do the job they were seeking. I was one of those people who simply didn't know what I needed to know—because no one had told me anything but "old wives' tales" about job hunting—and lost more opportunities than I can count as a result.

I want to thank all the experts, executives, and successful job-getters who graciously shared their tips, insights, and experiences with me as I researched this book. Through them, I discovered that job getting is the consequence of a carefully planned series of success-engineering actions which are both behavioral and psychological. This book is the result of a systematic personal marketing approach that I developed and taught as part of The Mentoring Network and currently through Effectiveness-Plus.

This book is also dedicated to all who benefited from this teaching and consultation by getting jobs they wanted and providing feedback to me on what worked especially well for them individually. A big thumb's up to their ongoing success ... and yours!

DEDICATION

TABLE OF CONTENTS

INTRODUCTION

Having the job you truly want—a job which is rewarding on many levels and brings out the best in you—isn't a fantasy. However, successfully finding and securing such a job, irrespective of the state of the economy or the job market, is so much more than simply knowing what you want in a job and matching it to a newspaper "want ad" or recruiter's "job description." And it's so much more than having someone tell you about a position or, if you're really lucky, put in a good word for you.

While knowing generally what you want and finding something that seems to match it is necessary, it is not sufficient. You need to determine, understand, and consider so much more before your write to a company's personnel department, make an application online at monster.com, talk to a decision maker, or set foot in an employment agency or headhunter's office to explore job-opening opportunities.

What this means is that getting a job you want is highly unlikely *unless* you know what you need to do in order to *prepare* for it ... then actually go through all the required steps involved in preparing for it.

This book takes you systematically, step-by-step, through the entire job-getting process from discovering the many less-obvious personal, job- and company-related factors that can come into play as you look for a position, then matching what you have and want against each job opening and company, to being offered the position and deciding if the offer is what you truly desire. Exercises, guidelines, tips, examples, and resources abound so you can know precisely what works and why and how to apply it to yourself.

Through its six comprehensive chapters, you will learn how to determine your true personal and job values and what you *really* want in a position that will match your expertise and experiences and satisfy your needs and desires.

You will learn how to research the job and company, its accomplishments and problems, in order to demonstrate that you understand what they need, can help them solve those problems, and have a bottom-line track record of results to *prove* what you claim in order to get the interview.

You will learn that what you've likely been taught about cover letters and résumés doesn't work in today job market. Instead, you'll discover an alternative approach to grab the decision maker's interest and provide him or her with how you specifically match their position and needs, meet their expectations, and can significantly benefit their bottom line. Everything you do will be geared to getting your foot in the company's door so you can dazzle them with your footwork in the interview and set you apart from the other job applicants.

You will learn in detail what is expected of you in an interview, how to present and promote yourself effectively to meet the interviewer's expectations of a "great hire," what to ask, how to answer, what to do and what not to do, when to do it, and precisely how to do it.

You will learn about the culture of business testing of job applicants, what testing means to the applicant, the types of employment tests that are being used, how to respond to them to fulfill the company's expectations of the perfect job candidate, and the important historical, ethical, and privacy considerations of testing.

Finally, you will learn when the job is offered what to consider, what to do (and what not to do) in response, and when to do it so that you get the best deal possible and professionally benefit yourself the most at that time.

1

WHAT ARE YOU REALLY LOOKING

FOR IN A JOB?

Getting a job is never as easy as it sounds to the uninitiated. Anyone who has ever embarked on this journey knows that the path to a job is often a slow, slogging trek on a muddy track, filled with rocks and roots to stumble over, and is fraught with many potential dangers. Before you begin this more accelerated journey toward your goal of securing the job you want, there are some well-established, effective guidelines to keep in mind as you navigate the process. You'll need to:

1. Decide what you want to accomplish in realistic, concrete, specific, and time-defined terms.
2. You have to be able to observe your results when you achieve them and measure your success.

3. Intend to achieve your success so you will publicly commit yourself to doing (no ifs, ands, or buts)

4. Determine every step in the step-by-step process

5. Determine how you will address each step

6. Determine what resources you will need to do it

7. Gather the resources to implement your plan

8. Keep thinking positively because you know it is physically possible to achieve your goal

9. Focus on achieving each successive step toward your ultimate goal, tweaking where necessary

10. Work hard, handle obstacles objectively, and never give up on achieving your dream.

ASSESSING YOUR TRUE WANTS

Before you can assess what you want in a job, you have to be sure you know what you have to offer to a job and a company. That is, you have to know what your strengths, attributes, skills, abilities, talents, values, preferences, likes, dislikes, desires, needs, attitudes, beliefs, and areas of expertise and experience are.

For you to make the most of your job search opportunities you need to decide specifically and precisely:

. What you want

. What you don't want

. What fits you best personality-wise, personally, socially, occupationally, and professionally to achieve your life goals now and in the future.

If this sounds like a lot of work, it is. But it is absolutely essential for you to know to get what you *really* want. You may, like most of us, have only an inkling initially of what you must know before you start your job-getting journey. Consequently, you will likely tend to want to rush headlong into doing what you've always been taught is the proper sequence of things: Decide what job you want, create a résumé and cover letter, get the interview, and accept the job offer. But, unfortunately, too often that unknowing, simplistic approach leaves you uninformed and unprepared. That is, you have not done what's necessary to think about *all* the important personal and company details, the possible consequences of the job or how you're conducting yourself to get it, and the potential implications for decision makers to whom you're presenting yourself.

Let's say the job for which you're applying has some understated supervisory or managerial components. The employment ad may not have emphasized it, you may have missed their inference, or you didn't do any outside research to see what that type of job in that company typically involves. Without that information, you don't have and can't consider the details, consequences, and implications of all the different aspects of the job. So you likely haven't thought about how you'd feel if you were asked to take over leadership on a moment's notice in a fast-paced environment ... or how the long hours and possible weekends might affect your personal time with loved ones or pastimes.

Once you've gone through the time, effort, and agony of the job-getting process, you don't want to finally accept something only to find it doesn't fit you in the most basic of ways. Granted, nothing is going to be "perfect," but you don't want it to grate on you or be unsatisfying or make you hate going to work. What this means is that:

1. You need to know as much as possible about yourself and the job.
2. You need to remove as many of the negatives ahead of time as possible.
3. You need to know where the compromises are likely to occur.
4. You need to know what compromises are acceptable short-term and long-term for satisfaction AND what are not.

The objective of being truly prepared is to give you the greatest amount of control in this important evaluation process—control over what you want and how your wants match what you have and what's available. Since YOU are the one to make the decision of what is more likely to work for you, you need to know intimately about yourself as if you were a product you were "selling."

WHAT ARE YOUR CORE CHARACTER STRENGTHS

Before you need to look at what your organizational strengths and abilities are, you need to discover what your personal core character strengths and virtues are. These are your positive traits and emotions that affect everything you do. They represent reservoirs of positive energy. They show what activities you are drawn to and your affinity for them. They indicate what will be easy for you to learn and apply. They suggest what energizes or frustrates you. Furthermore, they can buffer against misfortune and act as a positive motivator in all you do.

Knowing them means you can use them to become the best you can be in every aspect of your life because you can leverage them. Knowing them means you can develop satisfying relationships and a personal-work life balance. Knowing and applying them means you can create a pleasurable, engaged, meaningful, and rewarding life.

Your true strengths are what you can use to make yourself shine as a person and job applicant-then-candidate and differentiate you from all the other job applicants, candidates, and employees on the job.

EXERCISE
Your Core Character Strengths and Virtues

Go to (http://www.viame.org/) to learn what Positive Psychology has scientifically discovered over many years are your 24 core character strengths and virtues. The VIA Signature Strength Survey is a 240-question survey that has been taken by hundreds of thousands of people.

The six (6) values and twenty-four (24) character strengths are human traits valued in all cultures and religions around the world and are universally expressed across all areas of life, from home to family to social life to work. The six virtues under which are the twenty-four character strengths are: *Wisdom* and *Knowledge*; *Courage*; *Humanity*; *Justice*; *Temperance*; and *Transcendence*.

Your survey results page will show you your five (5) greatest character strengths. You can take this survey for *free*. Once you have taken the survey, you need to spend time asking yourself the following then record your answers:

1. How do I currently use my core strengths?

2. In what situations in the past have I used each of these strengths?
3. Where and when do I currently use each of them?
4. How do I feel when I use each of them?
5. How could I apply each of them at work?
6. How could I apply each of them in my job search?
7. How could I make each of them stronger?
8. How could I apply each of them to more aspects of my life?
9. What does "life satisfaction" mean to me?
10.What does "job satisfaction" mean to me?

What you want in a job tends to be much more complex than you might imagine. Knowing as much as you can about yourself and about a job and company of interest can help reduce the number of conflicts you experience in trying to get a job that lets you achieve what you want and do it comfortably.

Note: I strongly suggest you create an 8 1/2" X 11" notebook to put all your exercises, research results, thoughts, decisions, and other information in one place for ready reference and for constant updating.

EXERCISE
Your Organizational Skills and Abilities
You have many skills and abilities that you may not have thought about but that may be relevant to your successful your job-getting process. The following list will help you tease out your strengths:

WHAT YOU HAVE (Specify and Describe)

__ 1. Organize work to be done

___ 2. Identify problems that exist
___ 3. Analyze problems
___ 4. Establish priorities
___ 5. Set clear goals
___ 6. Brainstorm solutions to problems
___ 7. Evaluate alternatives as a solution
___ 8. Decide on an alternative as a solution
___ 9. Put your decision or that of others into effect
___ 10. Work with uncertain situations
___ 11. Improvise
___ 12. Foresee the consequences of these decisions
___ 13. Achieve goals despite obstacles
___ 14. Delegate responsibility to others
___ 15. Find information as needed
___ 16. Speak clearly and effectively
___ 17. Write clearly and effectively
___ 18. Listen, understand what is said
___ 19. State wants reasonably
___ 20. Express anger positively
___ 21. Relax, reduce tension
___ 22. Handle stressful situations calmly
___ 23. Accept criticism objectively
___ 24. Follow detailed instructions
___ 25. Complete tasks on schedule
___ 26. Experiment with new ideas
___ 27. Instruct, coach, advise others
___ 28. Supervise others
___ 29. Manage projects and people
___ 30. Give orders and stand behind them
___ 31. Evaluate others' work/contribution
___ 32. Motivate others into action
___ 33. Influence and persuade others
___ 34. Sell idea to decision makers

__ 35. Show understanding to others
__ 36. Give support to others
__ 37. Put yourself in other's shoes
__ 38. Get understanding from others
__ 39. Get support from others
__ 40. Access others for what you want
__ 41. Seek more projects and responsibilities
__ 42. Talk with strangers
__ 43.Give constructive feedback
__ 44. Give presentations
__ 45. Speak out at meetings
__ 46. Other

Now you need to go back to the above list pull out your *greatest* Organizational Skills and Abilities. Once you've made a list, you need to rank-order them in descending order, beginning with your greatest skill or ability and finishing with your great but lesser skills and abilities.

YOUR ORIENTATION: PEOPLE VS. DATA

In order to determine what area(s) would be the best to pursue, you need to do a further personal assessment. You need to look specifically at People-oriented skills and interests and Data-oriented skills and interests. Consider the following carefully:

1. *People with whom you prefer to work*:
   a. Number of people (individually vs. in groups)
   b. Work style (analytical vs. creative)
   c. Decision making (thoughtful vs. impulsive)
   d. Personality style (objective vs. subjective)
   e. Ethnicity/culture (specific groups)

f. Status (blue-collar vs. white-collar)

g. Power level (decision makers vs. subordinates)

h. Behavioral style (formal vs. casual)

2. *Skills you have and/or would like to use with people*:

a. Communicating - giving direction; exchanging information (verbal vs. written)

b. Advising - gathering information in order to give professional advice or recommendations

c. Managing - determining/ interpreting goals/procedures/ specific duties to individual/group, and at the same time helping to evolve harmonious relations, promoting efficiency–often through critical watching or evaluation, and/or feedback

3. *Data* - in general, knowledge, concepts, ideas, theories, facts, information with which you like to work

4. *Basic data* (accumulation of knowledge for its own sake) vs. applied data (use of information to address/improve a situation)

5. *Data dealing with people* - new approaches, solutions, sources, points of view, findings, conclusions, recommendations, plans, objectives, goals, tactical needs, needs, project goals

6. *Skills you have or would like to use with data*:

a. Analyzing - examining complex whole for components in order to evaluate data and/or present alternative actions, interpretations

b. Synthesizing - bringing into close relationship/combining/
uniting various groups or analysis of data into coherent whole/
complex unit so as to discover new facts, concepts, interpretations, directions, approaches

c. Coordinating - determining time/place/sequence of action/operation of process/system/organization, and/or need for revision of goals/policies - all based on analysis of data and/or a review of pertinent objectives/requirements. May include overseeing or executing decision reached.

7. *Your interests by topic area*: Activity Level

    a. Physical vs. non-physical

    b. Psychological (behavioral vs. cognitive vs. emotional)

    c. Experiences supporting your likes

8. *Areas that are strongly not of interest and your reasons for that.*

EXERCISE
Work Preferences

Go back to #1-8 of the previous exercise and spend at least an hour making lists in response to each numbered item and its sub-categories. Once you have done that, rank-order your lists in ascending order. That is, start with what is your strongest attribute, skill, or preference in that category and work toward your least strong attribute, skill, or preference. This should give you a core of what you prefer/like and what skills you feel most confident about.

WHAT ARE YOUR JOB PRIORITIES

Once you've assessed your skill, ability, interest, and preference areas for a job, you need to look more deeply into what it is you want your desired job to represent. The job needs to represent not only what you have to bring to it but also your values and your goals associated with those specific values.

You need to have a complete understanding of those

values so you can choose more precisely where and how you want to fit your interests, abilities, overall values, likes, dislikes, preferences, and strengths into a job. You further need to rank this information so you know which of your values take priority.

As you know, this is not an easy process. If it were, there wouldn't be so many seeking this information. There wouldn't be innumerable career counselors and career-oriented books offering you help.

HOW TO MAKE A WISER JOB DECISION

Making a wise job-getting decision requires a more thorough self-examination than just determining what abilities, expertise, and experience you have. You also need to be aware of:

. The choices you have
. Your preferences among the choices
. Their long-term effects on your goals, values, long-term desires, your career, life style, comfort, and your way of life.

The following are guidelines you can follow to help you evaluate your inner-most needs and the relative merits of job alternatives.

DO YOU WANT A BIG OR SMALL COMPANY

One basic question you need to ask yourself is, "Should I work for a big or small company?" This may seem like a non-question. But either choice has many important implications for you. Let's consider some of their dimensions and potential effects on you.

Risk versus security. A large company with $245

million in annual sales, in business for 30 years, will offer you more security than an entrepreneurial startup. You need to ask yourself in what environment you will feel more comfortable. You need to ask yourself in which environment will you likely function better. That is, do you prefer the security of a large, well-established firm or the risk and challenge of a small, innovative company, which is working with narrow margins?

Overall industrial outlook. If the industry as a whole is on the decline, it wouldn't make much difference what size organization you choose. If the industry is healthy and growing, you then need to ask what the company's standing is in that marketplace. Is it developing new products, increasing its annual sales, and receiving a reasonable return on investment? Or is it static? Company size won't mean much if the organization itself is stagnating, standing still on tried-and-true products rather than engaging in active research and development for future products and services and attracting even larger audiences.

You need to ask if the company is likely to become part of a merger or the object of a takeover attempt. These two scenarios create instability and dramatic change, and they are areas which should be avoided by all except thrill-seeking crisis managers.

Exposure and opportunity. In a small company you're likely to have greater exposure to senior management. As a result, you will likely have a greater opportunity for involvement with strategy. This means greater likelihood for recognition of your efforts. It also increases your chances to be creative.

In big companies, however, your role will likely be

more specialized and focused. Your responsibility will tend to be for one type of activity. Having this circumscribed position—one more distant from decision makers—makes both your efforts and accomplishments tend to be less visible, less recognizable. This, in turn, can render you somewhat "anonymous" unless you work hard at creating your own visibility and credibility. You have to assess whether you can feel fulfilled in a job where you function more as a *worker bee* and less as a driving force.

Personality and work style. Do you like working with a variety of tasks? Do you like the broad exposure afforded when you are and are seen as a generalist? You need to ask yourself if you can function effectively under the pressure inherent in the multi-task, multi-responsibility environment. Are you comfortable and confident accepting autonomy? Can you take the initiative? If so, a small, recently-established or entrepreneurial company may be for you.

Or, do you prefer a more structured environment with clearly defined tasks and responsibilities? Would you prefer to work at a somewhat slower pace with more supervision? Do you see yourself as more of a specialist, doing one thing very well rather than many things passably? If so, a large company may be for you.

Long- and short-term goals. Before you decide on pursuing only large or small companies, you need to ask yourself about your job goals. Do you want to progress at a steady rate over the years? That is, slowly collecting salary increases and, perhaps, promotions? Or, do you want to be on the fast track, rapidly moving up in title, power, and financial remuneration?

Where do you want to be in five years? In 10 years? If you want to be doing pretty much what you're doing now, but with more pay and/or more responsibility, the large company may be your environment. If, however, you want to be in control, shaping strategy and policy, helping the company grow, influencing profit, and reaping the benefits sooner than later, a small, innovative company may be your milieu.

By realistically assessing yourself and your job goals in terms of your values, needs, as well as your abilities and experience, you should be able to determine what organizational structure best meets your requirements. You can then set your sights on potential companies that match your preferred profile.

WHAT ARE YOUR PERSONAL VALUES

Your values are those qualities in yourself, others, situations, and jobs you find most attractive and meaningful in all you do in your life. You need to see how your values relate to the job goals you're trying to achieve. Some basic human values that you need to consider are:

. Recognition
. Security
. Affection
. Affiliation
. Approval
. Popularity
. Achievement
. Power
. Responsibility

. Belongingness
. Wealth.

EXERCISE
Work and Life Values

Answer each of the following using the values listed above. Answer as fully as you can, coming back to them as necessary:

1. What do you value in life? Why? (List all that are important.)
2. What are your three (3) most important personal values? Why?
3. What do you value in a job? Why? (List all that are important.)
4. What are your three (3) most important job values? Why?
5. Where do conflicts exist between your personal and job values? Why?
6. Where are there matches between your personal and job values? Why?
7. Describe your ideal job in your values (Be as detailed as possible.)
8. Describe your ideal workday in your values.
9. Describe your ideal boss in your values.
10. Describe your ideal value-based work-and-life balance (areas include work, personal, family, community).
11. List and rank in your own order of priority the following job values:
. Achievement
. Affiliation
. Approval
. Authority
. Challenge

. Creativity
. Fringe benefits
. Independence
. Interest
. Leadership
. Leisure
. Money
. Popularity
. Power
. Prestige
. Recognition
. Relationships
. Responsibility
. Reward
. Security
. Self-expression
. Service
. Status
. Time
. Variety.

12. Commit these values to paper and entitle it, "Values Important to Me." Place it somewhere in plain view, like on your computer monitor or the refrigerator, as a constant reminder.

WHAT ARE YOUR JOB VALUES

When you think about job targets, you need to think about what's important to you in a job.

What's *primary*?
. Using your skills?
. Demonstrating your experience?

. Being creative?

. Commuting distance?

. Opportunity for advancement?

. Level of responsibility?

. Money?

. Possibility for promotion?

. Company goals?

. Company philosophy?

. Company ethics?

What's *secondary*?

. Location?

. Company reputation?

. Job title and status?

. Perks?

You have to break this down for yourself with each job possibility.

EXERCISE

Job Value Assessment

Answer each of the following as fully as possible, coming back to it as necessary.

1. What do you do or are trained to do for a living?

2. To what degree are you continuing to develop those skills?

3. What kind of company or organization have you worked for before?

4. What did you like and dislike about it? Why?

5. What kind of company or organization do you want to work for now? Why?

a. Big?

b. Little?

c. Family-owned?

    d. Multi-national?

    e. For profit?

    f. Non-profit?

    g. College?

    h. Other academic institution?

    i. Association?

    j. Foundation?

    k. Government?

6. How do you want the company to relate to employees? Why?

    a. Care about employees—atmosphere of closeness?

    b. Not care about employees—atmosphere of distance?

7. Which is more important to you? Why?

    a. Quick advancement with no security?

    b. Slow advancement with security?

8. Which would you prefer? Why?

    a. Large national company with possibility of relocation?

    b. Small, local company with little possibility of relocation?

9. What kind of hours do you prefer? Why?

    a. High involvement—arrive early, leave late?

    b. Low involvement—essentially 9-to-5?

10. How do you feel about frequently having short deadlines? Why?

11. What kind of environment do you prefer? Why?

    a. Very competitive with opportunity for advancement?

    b. Less competitive with less opportunity for advancement?

12. How important is it for the company to have a social conscience? Why?

13. How important is it for the company to have concern for the environment? Why?

14. How important is it for the company to have concern about discrimination within the company (racism, sexism, ageism, sexual harassment, disabilities)? Why?

15. How important is it for the company to have concern about a quality product? Why?

16. What stability situation is more important? Why?
   a. Rapid expansion with instability?
   b. Slow expansion with stability?

17. What is the preferred number of employees in the company? Why?

18. Which do you prefer to work with: Product or service? Why?

19. Which do you prefer to work with: People or data? Why?

20. Which do you prefer: Work alone or in a group? Why?

21. What salary do you want in a new position? Why?

22. How does this salary desire compare with regional and industry-wide salary rates?

23. Would you settle for less salary in order to gain greater responsibility, challenge, or fringe benefits? Why?

24. How well do you tolerate job pressure?

25. Do you have coping mechanisms in place to handle stress?

26. How much job pressure are you willing to experience in your job? Why?

27. What do you want to accomplish through your job? (List all tangible and intangible goals.)

28. How comfortable are you interacting with others formally?

29. How comfortable are you interacting with others informally?

30. How comfortable are you giving reports to groups or authority figures?

31. How comfortable are you giving speeches when required?

32. How willing are you to engage in company politics?

WHY A VALUES' MATCH MATTERS

In today's very competitive world, you have to know as precisely as possible not only what you want but also what you *don't* want in a job. It's also important to remember that *taking just anything* for the money will likely work for only a while. Over time it will likely begin to chafe, leaving you feeling disgruntled, disappointed, and frustrated, perhaps even angry with yourself for doing it, even if you needed the money.

Whenever you can, you want to make the match as comfortable as possible. Feeling comfortable about your job fitting with your values will help you get through tough times and be even more productive. It will also help you promote yourself more effectively and persuasively because it *feels* right.

However, it's a fact of Nature that every job will be a compromise. It will have aspects you like, some you don't like, and some about which you feel neutral. It is essential that you maximize the positive job aspects and minimize the negative. To do this you need to not only match your preferences but also keep your values at the top of your thinking.

Of course, "compromise" means you'll have to go with a job that is a "good enough" fit to you and all that you bring personally and behaviorally to the job and company.

Warning: Never compromise your values. If your values feel "compromised," you will tend to dwell on that subconsciously if not consciously.

. It will gnaw at you.
. It will affect your mood.
. It will affect your attitudes.
. It will affect your level of job satisfaction.
. It will affect your performance and output.

. It will spill over into your personal life.

It's important to remember that over time your own personal and job values may shift. This can make some values either more or less important. It can re-arrange your priorities, what you want to achieve, how you want to achieve it, and how you feel about it.

Knowing this can happen makes it essential that you re-do this assessment occasionally to see if you are achieving your goals, if other goals are taking their place, and how satisfied you are with what you're doing, the job, and the company. Therefore:

. The better the initial match, the greater will be your chances for having less internal stress in your job.
. The better the initial match, the fewer your complaints will be about job tasks, responsibilities, compensation, and benefits.
. The better the initial match, the more likely you will take pride and will find satisfaction in what you do as well as in meeting your own personal goals.

Figuring out all the things you want in a job and where you are willing to compromise will help you find a matching job more easily and comfortably. And ultimately this will make you feel more confident, in control, and successful with respect to yourself, your job-getting process, and in the job you choose.

2

WHY DO I HAVE TO RESEARCH

THE JOB MARKET?

"Why do I have to research the job market? Why can't I just apply for jobs that seem to match my qualifications?" Of course, you CAN! And job-seekers do it all the time. But that's the problem if you want to significantly increase your chances of being successful.

If you're serious about finding a job that *really* matches you, in a company that is healthy and not contemplating changes, in an industry that is on the up-trend, you WON'T want to leave your hunting to Hope, Wishful Thinking, and Chance!

In a survey I did of over 800 randomly-selected business and professional people 78 % of them said they were struggling because they did not know how to gain access to the information, resources, and skills they needed to meet their personal job-getting and personal work goals.

What this suggests is that *if* you simply apply for jobs without doing your research, you are actually putting yourself at risk ... in harm's way. Because:

. You won't know what you need to know about the likely position.
. You won't know what is likely expected of you.
. You won't know about the company's philosophy and agendas.
. You won't know about the company's track record.
. You won't know the company's standing in the industry.
. You won't know the company's current and past problems.
. You won't know about its new products of services.
. You won't know about the decision maker.

What this all means is that you won't be able to effectively and efficiently present and promote yourself to the decision maker. Specifically, you won't be able to show in detail how your qualifications truly match the position. But, *most importantly*:

1. You won't be able to demonstrate that you know their issues.
2. You won't be able to demonstrate that you understand their problems.
3. You won't be able to demonstrate that you can help them solve their problems.
4. You won't be able to demonstrate that you can do it better than anyone else!

In any market, but especially in a tight and very competitive market, when you are the one who intimately knows the lay of the land, you are the one who has the *best* chance of rising above the other job-seekers to achieve your job-getting goal.

WHAT IMPRESSES DECISION MAKERS THE MOST

You need to ask yourself what impresses decision makers the *most*? The answer is individuals who present themselves as talented, knowledgeable, savvy professionals impress executives most. Specifically, it is job seekers who indicate that they:

. Want the job
. Understand the industry and company
. Understand the company's issues and problems
. Have a bottom line results' track record
. Have necessary data and people skills
. Are aligned with the company philosophy
. Can be versatile, flexible, and adaptable
. Will be a loyal team player
. Are concerned *only* about the *company's* bottom line.

Lillian Vernon, president and CEO of the Lillian Vernon Corporation, one of the nation's leading mail-order firms, once said that in choosing an employee it is chemistry that is important. This means both good people skills and understanding and fitting into the corporate culture in both personality traits and attitude.

Richard C. Bartlett, past-president and CEO of Mary Kay Cosmetics, has said that the best employees take that extra step. They're willing to put in extra time when it's needed. They're loyal team players.

So what has this to do with researching the market? It indicates that by reading business periodicals offline and online, for example, you can determine the philosophy and orientation of particular companies. You can know what they are thinking right now. That is, you can know ahead of time what Lillian Vernon Corporation or Mary Kay Cosmetics likely wants on a philosophical or interpersonal basis, which is something you would want to emphasize to them.

If you don't know the company—*really* know the company, you will hurt your chances of getting the job. It has been demonstrated that this is likely to occur in 75% of the interviews you encounter. By your researching the market you will discover where you have a common ground with a potential employer. When you know this, you can then show how you truly match their job requirements as well as their company philosophy and culture.

What kinds of matches do you want to show? You can show how you've been acquainted with:

. Same or similar business
. Similar products
. Similar services
. Same or similar position.

IMPORTANCE OF DETERMINING SIMILARITY

Similarity is important for any kind of attraction to take place.

Research on interpersonal relationships, especially

with respect to dating, has found similarity to be exceedingly important to make relationships more likely to occur. This applies to the employer and potential employee relationship as well. When there is similarity, there is attraction. When there is similarity, there is liking.

In other words, the greater the similarity there is the greater the attraction. The greater the attraction there is the greater the liking. Companies want their individuals, teams, and their culture as a whole to demonstrate similarity.

WHY DO JOB RESEARCH

"Still," you say, "I've never had to do research before so why should I have to do it now?" Good question. The answer is that if you're going for a lower-level job, when companies are desperate for employees, and the economy is good, you are more likely to get a job without a lot of time and effort spent in research and preparation. However, if you're looking for a higher-level job, when companies are being very selective, and/or the economy is less than ideal, you are unlikely to just slip into a position without researching the market in order to promote yourself most effectively as their perfect match.

In this scenario many more people who are qualified, with credentials equaling or better than yours, will be clamoring for that one particular job. Consequently, you had better have sound, solid ways to create positive visibility and credibility for yourself in the eyes of the potential employer. If you don't, you'll be just another face in the crowd jockeying to be seen and heard.

"Okay, but what is research *really* going to do for

me?" The answer is "Everything!"

Your researching the market takes a lot of the risk out of your job-getting gamble. The results of your marketing research efforts allow you to position yourself in keeping with:

. Industry trends
. Company trends
. Company structure and characteristics
. Company philosophy
. Company mission
. Company culture
. Company needs and desires
. Company products and services
. Company track record
. Company problems
. Company methods for achieving goals
. Company goals.

Your acquired understanding the company's problems enables you to identify and promote yourself as the solver of that specific company's problems. This will allow you to begin to move ahead of the pack of your competitors for that position. Furthermore, it gives you the confidence so necessary for your job-getting efforts because it can tell you almost everything that's important about the company, the job opening, and decision maker for it.

Your research will also help you further clarify your own goals as they pertain to what the company can offer. You're looking for a goodness-of-fit with the position and company and you are looking for ways you can demonstrate it to them. You'll be far more successful when you know specifically:

1. Where you're going?
2. Why you're going there?
3. How you're going to get there?

If you don't know these things because you're not fully and appropriately prepared, you'll undermine all your job-getting efforts. *Never forget*: Knowledge is power. Anything less than having this knowledge is just plain wishful thinking. And wishful thinking can never get you your job.

EXERCISE
Company Analysis

Marketing research information identifies the company's problems, needs, and wants. It begins with the analysis of the marketing opportunities associated with the industry and the firm of interest.

Pick an industry and firm within it (since this is practice, pick as easy an industry and firm as possible as you get used to doing this research), then answer the following questions as specifically and concretely as possible. This will give you a good idea of the kinds of information you need to be aware of and gather.

ENVIRONMENTAL ANALYSIS
1. What are the main trends within the industry? (Toward or away from that particular product or service?)
2. What are the main trends within the firm? (Toward or away from that particular product or service?)

3. What are the opportunities within the industry? (New technology, laws, mergers to support products or services?)

4. What are the opportunities within the firm? (New technology, laws, mergers to support products or services?)

5. What are the main threats within the industry? (New technology, laws, mergers that no longer support products or services?)

6. What are the main threats within the specific firm? (New technology, laws, mergers that no longer support products or services?)

DEMAND ANALYSIS

7. What is the current size of this market? (Number of sales locally, regionally, nationally, and internationally?)

8. What is the future size of this market? (Projected number of sales locally, regionally, nationally, and internationally?)

MARKETING SEGMENTATION ANALYSIS

9. What are the major companies making up this market? (Who are this company's direct competitors and how do they rank?)

MARKET ANALYSIS

10. What are the operating characteristics of this market? (What have the trends been for this specific market, whether retail, wholesale, research, or services?)

COMPANY BEHAVIOR ANALYSIS

11. What do these companies desire and seek in employees? (What characteristics do these companies look for? Conservatism, creativity, loyalty, dedication, independence, team work, interpersonal skills, analytical thinking, etc.?

This research takes a while to do initially. *The next section will guide you in <u>how to locate</u> the necessary information to answer the above questions.*

Once you have done this for one company and industry, you should do it, one at a time, for the companies that are of particular interest to you. If the industry is the same, you will simply repeat the industry information. But each company of interest will be different in many ways. As a result, each company needs to have its own file. In this file you will write notes, questions, anything significant as well as your responses to the next two (2) exercises.

MOST USEFUL DIRECTORIES

The following are the standard directories for the information you will need in general and for the above exercise:

<u>Standard & Poor's</u> *<u>Register of Corporations, Directors, and Executives</u>*. Most publicly-held companies in the United States are listed here, along with the names of key officers, number of employees, total sales, kinds of products and services each company provides, and addresses of corporate headquarters. There are also pages on geographic and Standard Industrial Classification (SIC) codes so you can look up by region of interest or type of industry.

<u>Thomas</u> *<u>Register of American Manufacturers</u>*. This detailed, somewhat ponderous reference contains catalogues and product descriptions of many firms.

<u>Dun & Bradstreet's</u> *<u>Million Dollar Directory</u>*. This three-volume set is very similar to Standard & Poor's but has three separate sections by which companies are listed. They include Alphabetical (white pages); Geographical by

state and city (yellow pages); and SIC codes (blue pages).

Dun & Bradstreet's *Billion Dollar Directory* (Corporate Families). While this directory doesn't list information on divisions of major companies, it does list subsidiaries, divisions, and indices through which you can find the parent company or divisions owned by the parent.

Dun & Bradstreet's *Middle Market Directory*. Similar to the *Million Dollar Directory*, this volume provides information on privately-held and smaller companies.

Dun & Bradstreet's *Directory of Corporate Executives*. This volume contains short biographies of senior management in large American corporations. It details both educational and business backgrounds, which may be very useful information for creating identification and similarities with them. You need to know the decision maker for the job opening of interest.

Important: Be sure to check with the company *before* you prepare a profile on a corporate member or contact that particular executive/decision maker. You need to make sure the person listed is still there, in the same position, and responsible for that job. You don't want to create a "wow"-campaign to demonstrate how similar you are to the decision maker only to find that that person is:

. No longer there
. No longer in that position
. Not responsible for hiring for that opening
—and the person you contact turns out to be totally dissimilar.

Ward's *Business Directory: Largest U.S. Companies*. Companies are listed by both SIC codes, geography, and by the company's chief executive officer (CEO). You need to make note that this person may or may not be the appropriate contact as the decision maker for the position you want. You NEVER want to assume.

Moody's *Manuals (Public Utilities, Industrials)*. These manuals provide information on sales and growth trends of companies.

Directory of Directories. Here the 30,000-plus U.S. directories which cover most industries are listed and described.

WHAT RESEARCH PROVIDES

Marketing research not only focuses but also directs your job-getting efforts. For example, in one year the *Directory of Massachusetts High Technology Companies* identified 2,750 companies that were employing over 527,000 people. Through study of the directory at that time, you might have learned that more than 78% of the state's high-tech firms employed fewer than 100 people. Nearly half of these companies were started after a particular date and were classified as "small companies."

Furthermore, most new hiring, according to this directory, was done by small and medium-sized companies. Most cutbacks in larger companies were at the middle- and senior-management levels. The directory showed that the high-tech industry was currently unsettled and unpredictable.

But it also reflected at that time the high-tech job trends in the making, such as:

. Computer manufacturing down but software development and distribution up

. Aerospace and defense down but medical and biotechnology up
. Computer services down but networking and communication up
. Test equipment stable but optics, vision, imagining, and online transaction processing up.

The effectiveness of your job search is limited only by the accuracy and appropriateness of the list of potential companies you devise. Therefore, before you contact a single potential employer, you need to devote considerable time to your research. This means going to the library and pouring over reference books and industry *and* business magazines and newspapers.

They can provide you with press releases, up-to-the-moment information, rumors, and even gossip. To learn what the company of interest wants the public, stockholders, the industry, and other companies to know about them, you need to go to a business school library or contact the company's public relations, public communications, and public information department. There will be more on this in a moment. While you can gather some of this same information online, I strongly urge you to start with an on-site library search.

WHAT TO IDENTIFY IN YOUR RESEARCH

You want to identify not only companies in a particular industry, area of interest, geographic area, or a particular profession but also their executives. You need their names, titles, addresses, and telephone numbers. You can begin by asking the reference librarian to direct you to the business reference volumes mentioned above.

USEFUL OFFLINE SOURCES

These sources often reveal inside information about a company that you absolutely *must* know. The better you can demonstrate your knowledge and an "insider's" appreciation for the company, the better and more closely you can demonstrate how your qualifications match their criteria for the position.

Once again, you need to know the basics about a company:

1. Problems (internal and external)
2. Changes (any aspect of the business or its people, positive and negative)
3. Crises (law suits, financial or stock upset)
4. Growth (expansion where and under what circumstances)
5. Sales (increase or decrease)
6. Trends
7. New products
8. New services
9. Decision makers (promotions, awards)
10. Philosophy of how things should be done
11. Mission (what they hope to accomplish)
12. Internal policies and attitudes about personnel (positive and negative)
13. Perspective (how it views ethics, quality of product, consumers)
14. Responsibility (company as part of a larger community/environment)
15. Goals (bottom line, expansion)
16. Agenda (how to achieve those goals).

USEFUL ONLINE RESOURCES

You should do your research offline *first* to get your basic information most quickly. Then when you begin your *online* search, start with the following examples. But, don't stop there. Do you own online search on "business directories" and on periodicals for other useful references and articles.

Important: Each profession has its own "who's who," so don't forget to search by profession and names within that profession as well:

. *ZoomInfo* helps you find profiles of people, companies, tools, resources http://www.zoominfo.com/
. *Hoovers* is a Dun & Bradstreet company which provides information on people, companies, industries by company name and geography.
http://www.hoovers.com/
. *U.S. Business Directory* http://www.selectory.com/
. *Directories USA* http://www.directoriesusa.com/
. *U.S. Company List Database.*
. *Reference USA* http://www.referenceusa.com/
. *Business Search Engine and Business Directory*
http://www.business.com/

LOCAL RESEARCH

Each state has its own directories of business, industries, and manufacturers. Whenever you use these references be sure to use the most current volume. You will tend to find these in your metropolitan city library.

For companies in your geographic region, you should also check:

. Area employer directories
. Area employment agencies
. Executive search directories
. City business magazines
. Chamber of Commerce publications
. City industrial directories.

To gather in-depth information about specific companies in which you are most interested, don't forget to locate the company's annual report. As I said, you can find these at business college libraries as well as directly through the company itself. Check to see if you have any business colleges in your area and inquire about their holding of annual reports. Annual reports are reports to stockholders issued by publicly-held companies.

As I mentioned, don't forget the public relations department of the company. This information will likely include copies of articles about the company as well as descriptions of products, services, and company executives, their accomplishments, and other activities.

Once you have narrowed down your list of companies you want to pursue, you need to see what has been published about them—other than what you have received from the company's PR department. You will likely find more relevant business periodicals in your business college library, but your big city library may have them too. You can check for article entries about the company or executive in:

. _Business Periodicals Index_
. _Funk & Scott Index to Corporations and Industries_
. _New York Times Index_

. *Wall Street Journal Index* (which includes *Barrons Index*)
. *Public Affairs Information Services Index*
. *Readers Guide to Periodical Literature* (more general).

OTHER PRINT RESOURCES

You will often find hints of other places to look from the business directories and business publications. Helpful miscellaneous resources include:

. Newspaper libraries
. Advertising firms
. Public relations firms
. Stock brokers
. Management consultants
. Bankers
. Attorneys
. Fortune 100 listing
. Fortune 500 listing
. Fortune 1,000 listing
. Government agencies
. Internet searches
. The Free Library http://www/thefreelibrary.com/
. Business periodicals such as:
   - *Financial World*
   - *Forbes* *http://www.search.forbes.com/*
   - *Fortune* http://www.money.cnn.com/magazines/Fortune/Fortune_archive
   - *Business Week* http://www.businessweek.com/search.htm
   - *Barrons*

- *Financial World*
- *Advertising Age*
http://www.highbeam.com/Advertising+Age/publications.aspx?date=200310
- *PC Week* http://www.pcmag.com/
- *Industry Week*
- *Inc.* http://www.inc.com/magazine/
- *Success*
http://www.onlinesuccessmagazine.com/archive.php?=4

Important: I can't emphasize enough that you want to and need to demonstrate to potential employers that you are in sync not only with the field and industry in general but also with the company in particular, in detail. This is not to say that you are masquerading as an expert. You are presenting yourself as knowledgeable enough to fit with their company and, most importantly, *hit the ground running in the position.*

EXERCISE
Company Information

Once you have picked your primary companies of interest and created a file for each with all the basic information you have collected from the first exercise, you need to make sure you have gathered as much information from the offline and online references as possible to enable you to describe the company in the terms you've already seen listed. Use this as double-check list:

. Problems
. Changes
. Crises

. Growth
. Sales
. Trends
. New products
. New services
. Decision makers
. Philosophy
. Policies
. Perspective
. Agenda.

CLASSIFIED AD INFORMATION

While ads are not the best way to get a job, accounting for only 17% of hirings on average in *good* times, classified ads *can* provide you with considerable information. They tell you the types of positions that are typically found in the various fields and companies. They often detail position responsibilities and pay scale. They use jargon appropriate to the position—jargon which you must understand for the company and job. As a result, they often give you some sense of the company's organization and philosophy.

One of the best places to find useful classified ads in the Sunday Edition of major metropolitan newspapers, such as:

. *Boston Globe* http://www.boston.com/jobs/
. *Los Angeles Times*
http://www.latimes.com/classified/jobs/
. *Chicago Tribune*
http://www.chicagotribune.com/classified/jobs/
. *New York Times* http://wwwJobsOnline.net/.

Get them in print editions, where still available, or online. These papers carry ads from their immediate location, outlying areas, and from across the country because of their large readership.

Some papers are devoted specifically to job ads:
.The *National Business Employment Weekly* http://www.marineonstcroix.com/job/all_nbew.htm

You need to collect ads from classified ads from around the country and list them by job type.

Note: Please keep in mind that website addresses can and do change so at any given time they may no longer be accurate.

WHAT A "JOB LISTING" MEANS

Job listings do not necessarily represent a real open position. That is, the position might not really be open to the public. Many large companies hire from within but may be required to publicly post their openings. In this case, while there may be an opening, you may have no chance at getting it unless you're already their employee.

Classified ads may be run by an employment agency to drum up clients. They may be run by the company's own public relations department to create an image of growth. And they may be merely an attempt to keep the company visible against competition. The upshot is that you should use the information you find in ads as part of your research but should *not* count on any one "opening" to be a true opening for which you can apply.

Getting inside information from others—that is, word of mouth—is a much better way to know of a real opening. Be sure to talk with those you know. If you don't currently network, start networking, sharing your knowledge and expertise for what others can tell you.

Also check out state or city job fairs or career fairs where companies present information about themselves and opportunities with them. They also may take résumés from those attending. However, handing out your traditional résumé (that is, an un-researched, non-job-specific résumé) will likely be a big waste of time and energy. Still, if you can create a positive first impression when meeting the company's representative to make you more memorable, you may be able to reinforce that at another time (when there is a specific position you have researched) by referring to it.

Note: If you're considering going to a recruiting or staffing company, you need to keep in mind that they do *not* work for you. In fact, they work for the company which has an opening. While they will try to fit you with a job, they are not looking out for you. You are not their priority. So the fit may be less customized than you would like. I have experienced being sent out for interviews that were unrelated to what I was really seeking.

DON'T FORGET ASSOCIATIONS

Trade or professional associations are a valuable resource. They often hold meetings where you can network. You can find directories of them in your metropolitan library and sometimes online. They include:

. *Encyclopedia of Associations*
http://www.library.hbs.edu/go/encassoc.html
. *National Trade Associations of the U.S.*

. _Who's Who in Association Management_
. _Trade Association Directory_
. _The Association Directory_
http://www.recruitersnetwork.com/resources/associatio
ns.htm

Associations may also have newsletters which describe industry innovations and membership accomplishments, list job openings, and give brief member biographies. Newsletters of the companies of interest will tell you about:

1. Ongoing projects
2. Decision makers' names
3. Upcoming positions
4. New products and services
5. Policies, procedures, and philosophy of the company.

You can find company newsletters listed in:

. _IMS Ayer Directory of Publications_
. _Standard Periodical Directory_
http://www.mediafinder.com/
. _Oxbridge Directory of Newsletters_
. _National Directory of Newsletters_
. _Reporting Services and Newsletter Yearbook/Directory_
. _Newsletters Directory—Over Every Topic._
http://www.newsletteraccess.com/

For more information on newsletters, do an online search on the phrase "newsletter directories."

EXERCISE
Creating a Company Profile

Add any additional information you have gathered from these additional resources listed above on each company of interest to create a comprehensive profile. As a good candidate for the position, you are expected to not only demonstrate your knowledge of the company but also ask relevant questions about the job.

Determine what questions you want to ask in an interview. (Important questions to ask are included in the chapter on Interviews.) Decide how you will show that your qualifications match with as much of the job profile as possible.

CHECK COMPANY WEBSITES

Be sure to visit each company's website because this represents the information that each individual company believes is important to create the perfect image of what it is and what it does. As you check out the various website pages, make note of the _keywords_ they use in all their descriptions of themselves, from philosophy to services or products. These represent the image they want the public to see and accept. You will want to slip these keywords into your statements and answers to questions in your interview.

THE IMPORTANCE OF NETWORKING

Networking is an essential tool to find out more information about the marketplace, specific companies, and specific decision makers. While everyone has heard of networking, many people avoid engaging in it because they mistakenly believe it to be *using* people or trying to sell them something. On the contrary, *real* networking is all about sharing and helping. It is the active process of exchanging information with others in order to build and maintain relationships.

The result of networking is a team of supportive members to whom you can provide informational, instrumental, and emotional assistance and from whom you can receive the same when needed. Networking is built on the principle of *reciprocity*. Participants in a relationship expect to give as well as receive. If there is no mutual benefit, the interaction will feel unsatisfying and incomplete and likely cease.

You have a basic network of contacts of family, friends, colleagues, associates, and service people. It has been suggested that if you know fifty people on a first-name basis and so do all the people you know, you have available 2,500 friends of friends. The more friends you have, the greater the number of people exponentially to whom you have access.

You are likely to be more successful in networking and creating opportunities for yourself if you build your networking contacts with *two* goals in mind. The first is to make yourself well-known by providing assistance to others in need, and doing so *without* expectation of reward. The second is to have a specific goal in mind for which you are seeking assistance. Erroneously, people tend to equate only the second one with networking and then act on that alone.

Of the two, however, volunteering help is by far the more important because it fosters good will, expands your sphere of influence, and creates a positive impression of you. You go one step beyond and do more than just what is required or expected. Furthermore, you need to do so without any ulterior motive. That is, you are helping because you want to share, not because you desire a *quid pro quo* for it. This whole-hearted altruism engenders a sense of trust and gratitude in those with whom you network.

But to be this valued resource to your network you have to know what strengths and resources (skills, attributes, abilities, experience, information, connections) you have to offer. Humility and modesty can act as obstacles in this assessment. You must see yourself as having strengths that others want and value from which others can and will benefit.

To find business networks you would need to check the business section of your newspaper or online to locate networking groups in your field (such as relevant associations) and geographic area and their schedule for networking meetings. Likewise, belonging to business social media sites, such as LinkedIn (http://linkedin.com), can be very useful. There are different groups representing different professions where people exchange information and experiences, ask and answer questions. You may be able to locate what you need much more quickly from them and do it from the comfort and convenience of your home.

The more people who know about you, your expertise, lengthy experience, and *what you want*, the faster you can learn what you need to know and/or connect with a useful resource. You may even be able to locate inside information on job openings or a mentor who can act as guide and coach in exchange for your helping him or her.

As Henry David Thoreau once said, "If you have built

castles in the air, you need not be lost; that is where they should be. Now put the foundations under them." You do it with *real* networking!

DON'T SHORT-CUT

Even though you would probably like to get through this process as quickly as possible so you can start to work on your résumé and ready yourself for interviews, <u>do NOT give this research-based preparation short shrift</u>.

This is the *most basic and most important* part of your job-getting campaign once you have determined what you want and need in order to achieve your goals. You cannot match your abilities, expertise, and experience to a company, a decision maker, and a job if you do not know anything about them.

Think of yourself as a product you want them to buy. To make yourself as attractive to them as possible, you have to know precisely what they want so you can convince them you can give it to them—in spades. If you can satisfy their "What's in it for me," you can make yourself an outstanding candidate, distancing yourself from the pack. This approach really works and you'll be glad you took the time to do your job-market research.

3

CREATE A RÉSUMÉ BUT DON'T

SEND IT OUT?

You have been told it's important to create a résumé of your work experience to give to potential employers even before you know all about the job. But ... what you haven't been told is how to create a truly interpersonally-effective, on-target representation of your *most relevant* accomplishments, how they match the job requirements, *and* precisely how and when to share it with decision makers.

The *unfortunate truth* is if you give potential employers an <u>in</u>effective résumé, you may just *kiss* any chance of a job interview good-bye! So, what can you do about it?

. You can rethink what a résumé is supposed to be.
. You can recognize what a résumé really needs to represent.

. You can see a résumé from the potential employer's perspective.
. You can discover how to fashion a résumé so it will show you in your best light against your competition for that interview.

As you know, every employer expects you to have a résumé. It is traditional. We've been told that they want a formal summarization of *all* that you've done. As a result, we tend to think of a résumé as made up of the many threads of our experience, skills, and expertise that have been woven through our different jobs.

The problem is that a traditional résumé is highly unlikely to get the decision maker's attention, focus on your match to the job specifications, and create a positive first impression. Furthermore, it can't set the stage and present and promote you early in the process. For this reason you need to know:

1. How to create an achievement inventory
2. What elements are essential to promote
3. Interpersonally-effective formats and scripts to follow for each step in the process
4. Tools to match the "real" job requirements
5. How to immediately rivet the decision maker's attention and grab his or her interest
6. How to significantly increase the likelihood of your getting an interview
7. How your résumé can be the script for your interview that will make you stand out from the crowd
8. How to use your résumé to keep the glowing embers alive after your interview.

This means you have to know how to recreate the traditional résumé into an intriguing, promotional document to get the interview.

THE RÉSUMÉ ASSUMPTION

The assumption of most job getters is that once you present your résumé, which is your baby, someone at the company to which you have applied will carefully, thoughtfully, and lovingly read through this document. In doing so, they will enthusiastically discover, interpret, and connect the many disparate threads that make up your job-relevant fabric as they apply it to the specific job for which you have applied.

But, think about it for a moment. If you really tell them *everything* you've ever done, no matter how irrelevant to the job application or your desired self-presentation, what really will happen? Whoever reads it will become bogged down in the density of it—like getting stuck in mud.

Will they see the important job-specific threads among all the others—the wheat among the chaff? Will they be able to and willing to take the time to disentangle them from all the others? Will they make the appropriate connection between all you've done and the specs of the job for which you're applying? Or will they say, "This is a disorganized, unfocused mess"? With all this in mind, how likely is it they can see you as the best fit for the current opening?

This raises the BIG question: Should you provide such a general, all-encompassing, seemingly unfocused document to apply for specific jobs? The answer is a resounding, "No!"

NEVER SEND A TRADITIONAL RÉSUMÉ

Never send out a traditional résumé? That goes against everything you've ever been told about seeking jobs. So what does that mean? It means that what you really need to have in place of a traditional résumé is a document which provides *only* what is specifically and concretely *relevant* to the job for which you are applying.

In other words, it is only those qualifications—the jobs, experiences, expertise, skills, education, knowledge, and demonstrable results—you have had that are truly supportive and meaningful in the context of this *particular* position and its requirements. Specifically, this is *not* just for *any* position in your area of interest and expertise with *any* company.

This means you really need is to have a document that actively says what you've done and shows concretely its impact on a company's bottom line AND how that pertains to this particular company and this specific position for which you're applying.

You need to create a narrow document you can tailor and re-tailor to match you with each individual job opening. That is, it needs to be something that:

. Captures the reader's attention
. States what you've done that's relevant
. Focuses *specifically* on the potential position for which you hope to be a candidate
. Matches your strengths with company's job requirements.

The problem: The traditional résumé simply can't do this for you. So, if the traditional résumé does not promote you to a company, what does? Then what is the real purpose of the traditional résumé?

Its purpose is as a *personal worksheet.* It is for you alone to see. Its purpose is to help you define what you want and have to give to an employer in a specific company for a specific job. It is the initial blueprint for your job-getting campaign plan. This all-encompassing document should act only as a *resource* document for you. From it you choose what's important and necessary for each individual job application match. And, don't forget, that may differ significantly with each position for which you apply.

As a resource, it has within it the makings of an inventory of every specific thing you've ever done that *could* be relevant for any particular job opening. From it you gather and pick the items and threads that create and support your image as an effective and profitable performer in that job-application-related area of expertise and experience. However, you will need to bear in mind that each application will require a slightly different emphasis depending upon the company, its ideology, and public presentation.

The items and threads you choose from your inventory need to show a *progression* of your skills, talents, experience, expertise, and results in a particular area that the reader will find interesting, intriguing, and on-target for his or her specific job opening. Anything that does not reinforce or support that progression is filler which can distract the human resources person or decision maker from the overall point you're trying to make. You need to focus on what is necessary and sufficient for being considered for that job prominent so it can be spotted easily and quickly.

Something significant and essential that the traditional résumé does NOT do is demonstrate the *benefits* to the prospective company they would derive from hiring you. Traditional résumés don't give any of the measurable, quantifiable results you've achieved that support your qualifications as a productive performer. This leaves the prospective company without any sense of the results that you could achieve for them and how you could positively affect their all-important bottom line.

It's essential for you to start to think like a prospective employer: what they want and need and whether you can give it to them. *In the job-getting process it's NOT really about you.* (I'll state this repeatedly throughout the upcoming chapters in order to embed the notion that this is the harsh job-getting reality.) *It's all about the company and your answering THEIR question: "What's in it for me" in considering and hiring you.*

But, you might be wondering, if you threw out all the non-essentials in a traditional résumé, making it more relevant for a particular position, would the traditional résumé then do the job of promoting and representing you as you need it to do? Unfortunately, the answer is still No! The problem is also that a traditional résumé is a static and lifeless list of facts. It is only the bricks and mortar of your job-getting campaign. It is the foundation upon which you will build your job-getting *self-promotion*. But the traditional résumé is *not* your self-promotion—your story—by itself.

That is, it *does not <u>actively</u> and <u>vividly</u> tell your <u>unique</u>*

story *in terms of how you can help the company fulfill its desires based upon what you already have done.* In other words, the traditional résumé is unlikely to help single you out from all the other talented competitors for the position. It is unlikely to grab the company by the collar and rivet them to see how you are *the* match for them because it doesn't mold the desired image, attract the reader's attention, create desire for you, and encourage the employer to take a specific action on your behalf.

TRADITIONAL RÉSUMÉ IS A RESOURCE ONLY

Instead of sending out your traditional résumé, you use it to:

1. Determine your strengths in specific areas
2. Find important threads throughout your experience
3. Decide what your most impressive and relevant results have been
4. Create anecdotes about what you've done that will show the company your productivity and results.

From your traditional résumé you create a *functional* inventory. These are the relevant activities you have performed that will interest the company. By seeing what functions you have performed and which of these functions go together, you can realize exactly how your experience and education relate to the job you're seeking. This inventory can give you a good sense of the sequence of your progress to date that the company will find informative and impressive.

From this inventory you would pick *only* those functions that may be applicable to each specific position in each specific company. Always think of each job opening and each company as individually separate from the rest because they are: in how they do things, treat employees, what they think, and what they value.

So your functional inventory of relevant items is what you will use as the broad basis of your job-seeking campaign. It will be your constant reference. Specifically, it is what you refer to in your letters to prospective employers. (Yes, you'll be writing to employers!) It is what you will refer to when you talk about yourself in writing, on the phone, and in an interview. It is the basis of your interview script. However, it is NOT what you send out to anyone. At least, *not in its current form!*

Remember: When you let a potential employer know about you, you want to immediately direct their attention to how closely you fit their needs and wants. Bear in mind, however, their needs and wants include not only their specific job requirements but also your matching with their company's image, philosophy, mission, and goal and how they want to achieve their organizational goal.

To do this you first need to clearly demonstrate your benefits to them. You need to clearly show how you're *the* solution to the company's problem. What this means, of course, is that to know this you will have *researched* what their specific problems are and what is relevant for them. Remember, however, that relevance is a matter of degree and emphasis. This means you will need to create a document that you can and will constantly customize to each specific company and each specific position, reflecting their own particular degree and emphasis of relevance.

All of this is way before you contact anyone in writing about the job. Your first contact with the prospective employer will not be with your résumé but with a letter, an *action letter*. But that's getting a little ahead of the sequence of things in this process. First you need to turn your traditional résumé into a functional inventory.

EXERCISE
Summarize What You've Done

1. Summarize your experience on paper as a traditional résumé, first as a chronological résumé, second as a functional résumé, or inventory.

    a. <u>Chronological</u> gives your Education, Professional Experience by year, starting with the most recent job first.

    b. <u>Functional</u> gives your Education and Professional Experience by categories of type of work activity, such as "Training," "Managing," "Evaluating," "Designing," et cetera.

2. List all the activities and skills you used in each job in detail.

3. Take as much time as necessary. Don't rush. Keep going back and refining your entries.

4. This refinement will act as the basis of your job-getting promotion campaign. This means you need it to be as accurate and representative as possible.

RÉSUMÉ ISN'T REALLY ABOUT YOU

As you put together these two résumé formats, keep in mind that while you're writing about yourself, you are really writing to and *about* your prospective employer, which, in most cases, will be a for-profit business.

With this in mind, you need to ask yourself what is the main concern of a for-profit business? It is making a profit, of course. Therefore, for you to appeal to them you *must* show that prospective employer how you can help effectively and efficiently *solve their problems in order to help them achieve that profit.* Your research should have given you at the very least an inkling of their problems, desires, and current economic status.

Since it's all about *their* profit, it doesn't matter how brilliant, well-educated, or well-groomed you are, where you went to school, or for whom you worked (these are, of course, important), *if* you can't demonstrate how your performance in the past has added to productivity, and, thus, to profit (the bottom line) for others, and *will continue* to do so in the future for a new employer.

While you will later employ the chronology of the specific accomplishments you choose to emphasize, what you need to concentrate on first is your creating those functions in your inventory. To get your functional inventory to reflect this performance-profit connection, you need to put yourself in the shoes of the employer. Then ask yourself:

. What would your concerns be as an employer looking to hire someone for this particular position?
. What important strengths would you look for in an employee in general and in this particular position?
. How would you know a good candidate for the specific position if you saw one?
. What are your criteria for judging?
. What problems are you looking for a candidate to help the company and you solve?

The most successful self-promoting job-seekers put

themselves in the *minds of their target audience* who is the position's decision maker. They do that by thinking in terms of the decision maker's motivations, needs, and wants. This means you need to have done your research not only on the company but also on the decision maker so you can know her or him well enough to comfortably adapt your self-promotion documents and self-presentation to him or her.

Take a look at the functional résumé you created. How have you expressed your experiences, activities, and skills—your functionality? If you were following the traditional résumé format, you would probably just list your functions simply, such as: "I trained managers in communications." "I evaluated a communications program." But that's not particularly informative. Why? Because it doesn't really say what you did. So you need to ask yourself, if I were a potential employer, would that demonstrate to me that you have me, my company, and our bottom line in mind?

1. Do those functions demonstrate both a similarity and match?
2. Do those functions say exactly what I did and why?
3. Do those functions show my activities as being work-driven and relevant?
4. Do those functions show the results that were productively achieved?
5. Do those functions show a profit-centered consciousness?

Sadly, the answer is, "No." Not yet.

FUNCTIONAL INVENTORY DOS AND DON'TS

The first thing then you need to do is start to write each function as a single concrete deed, complete with the actions you performed. Since the *function* is what is important, you need to drop the "I" (as in "I did...") and replace it with a bullet point. It's not about you personally. It's about your behavior.

Then you would begin each bullet with an action verb. For example, you might start by saying, "Evaluated the company's communications program." But what does that mean? What was the purpose of the program? To be more descriptive and meaningful, you would then elaborate by saying, "Evaluated the company's communications program which was designed to fast-track middle managers." That's better detailed but it says very little that's useful to the decision maker in order for him or her to understand what you actually *did*.

You need to make it even *more* definitive to create a vivid word picture. You need to create a *scenario*. For example, you might add further details to come up with this: "Evaluated the company's interpersonal communications program designed to boost emotional intelligence skills and fast-track middle managers." That says a lot more about what you did. But while better, it *still* isn't enough.

What you need now is to *measure* those deeds. You do that by *quantifying* your *results* specifically and concretely. For example, you might write, "Evaluated Fortune-500 company's 150-person interpersonal communications program designed to boost emotional intelligence skills and fast-track middle managers over three years." This is even better, more detailed, and relevant. But something is still missing.

This bulleted sentence fragment requires one more element: the *practical, meaningful, profit-centered results of your actions* for your company. For example, adding your results, you would say, "Evaluated Fortune-500 company's 150-person interpersonal communications program designed to boost emotional intelligence skills and fast-track middle managers over three years, *resulting in a 20% increase in productivity.*"

That's much better! You showed what you did, the reason you did it, and the results of your actions. Of course, depending upon your field and prior jobs, it may be more difficult to demonstrate the quantifiable results. But, irrespective, you need to get as close as you can to it. (Other examples will follow.) You need to relate your previous results in some way that suggests a future repetition, positive benefit for the company to which you're applying.

EXERCISE
Deciding What to Include

How do you decide, of all the things you've done, what to put down?

1. Think in terms of the accomplishments of which you are most proud
2. Think in terms of what the employer is looking for—results that reflect profit-consciousness, such as:
   a. Increased sales
   b. Increased profits
   c. Increased productivity
   d. Increased efficiency

e. Saved money

f. Saved time

g. Reduced turnover

h. Reduced costs.

3. Be as specific and concrete as possible, using numbers. Generalities are uninformative and carry no impact whatsoever.

4. Think in terms of being able to visualize the sequence of events in vivid and meaningful detail.

POWER WORDS TO PAINT PICTURES

What words should you use? You want to express your message clearly, concisely, and quickly. But you also want to use words that paint an oil painting on canvas that the decision maker would want to hang in her or his office to impress organizational members and clients. This is a picture of what successful people in your field and in this specific position not only do but also are *expected* to do.

The following are examples of *Action Verbs* you should use because they have more punch and accuracy in describing what you did:

accelerated	accomplished	achieved	adapted
addressed	administered	advised	alerted
analyzed	anticipated	appraised	approved
arbitrated	arranged	assembled	assisted
attracted	audited	authored	built
calculated	catalogued	charted	checked
closed up	collected	compiled	completed
composed	compounded	conceived	concluded
conducted	conferred	confined	conserved
consolidated	constructed	consulted	contracted

contributed	controlled	cooperated	coordinated
corresponded	counseled	created	criticized
decreased	delegated	delivered	demonstrated
detected	determined	developed	devised
diagnosed	diagrammed	directed	discovered
disseminated	distributed	doubled	edited
effected	eliminated	enhanced	enlarged
established	evaluated	examined	exceeded
expedited	facilitated	fashioned	forecasted
formulated	founded	funneled	gathered
generated	governed	grouped	guided
harmonized	headed	identified	illuminated
illustrated	implemented	improved	increased
indexed	influenced	informed	initiated
innovated	installed	instituted	instructed
introduced	invented	investigated	launched
lectured	led	logged	made
maintained	maximized	minimized	moderated
modernized	modified	motivated	navigated
negotiated	obtained	operated	optimized
ordered	organized	originated	overhauled
oversaw	participated	performed	persuaded
pinpointed	planned	positioned	prepared
prescribed	presented	procured	produced
promoted	provided	published	realized
received	recommended	reconciled	recorded
rectified	reduced	refined	reinforced
reorganized	replaced	reported	represented
researched	reshaped	restored	revamped
reviewed	revised	revitalized	routed
safeguarded	saved	scheduled	scoured
secured	selected	served	serviced
set up	shaped	simplified	slashed
sold	solved	sorted	sparked

speeded up	staffed	started	simulated
streamlined	strengthened	structured	studied
suggested	supervised	tested	tied together
took charge	took over	trained	transacted
translated	triggered	tripled	upgraded
used	verified	wrote	

The great thing about well-chosen *action words* is that they can:

. Grab attention and direct the reader's focus
. Create a positive impact
. Stress your competence
. Indicate your ability to handle details
. Reflect your intelligence
. Reveal your management ability
. Show your profit-orientation
. Demonstrate your generalist abilities
. Demonstrate your specialist abilities
. Make you stand out behaviorally from other candidates.

RELEVANT ACCOMPLISHMENTS

The following are examples of how you might phrase your experience, showing concrete and specific detail, quantification, and bottom line-related results when they're available:

. Designed three-year soft-sell marketing program for action-adventure games software firm which increased sales 45%.
. *Designed* three-year soft-sell marketing program for action-adventure games software firm to increase sales 45%. (If you did not actually get the results of what you

did, for various reasons, you can re-phrase it. This at least shows how you planned the activity and what you expected to achieve.)

. *Developed* a six-module productivity-enhancement incentive program for assembly line workers which reduced turnover by 20%.

. *Created* layout and copy for 10,000-physician national direct mail pharmaceutical package on surgical use of eye ointment (where you don't have the specific results).

. *Produced* news releases for 225 speakers and exhibitors for SBANE conference which increased attendance 33%.

. *Redesigned* eight-page, four-color brochure for international semiconductor trade show in Japan on-time and under-budget.

. Increased visibility for new financial planning firm 66% via local media, special community events, and 800-number phone financial tips.

. *Operated* home-cleaning services with six full-time employees for six years at 21% profit.

. *Increased* weekly billings of regional event-planning business from 800 to 2,100 over two years for an increase of 262%.

RÉSUMÉ PRESENTATION ON PAPER

As mentioned before, you need to use bullets. This is because they force you to use keywords instead of long-winded sentences which can bury your results. These are quicker, easier, and snappier to read and understand than full sentences. They do away with fillers so they can emphasize your *go-getter's action.*

By eliminating the repetitive "I," you eliminate the sound of egocentrism. Instead, you make the *action,* not you, the center of attention. You direct the decision maker's mind toward matching your actions with the actions the decision maker has in mind for the desired position.

Each fragment should be long enough to create the picture but short enough to be read quickly. Average length of 10—20 words is best. But these can be a bit longer where absolutely necessary to conjure up the image you want. This means that you need to make sure each word conveys precisely what you want it to as succinctly as possible. As you can see, there is no fluff allowed.

WHAT TO AVOID SAYING

Look back at each example above. Note that each is an *objective* statement of deeds. Each is a fact, not an opinion or judgment. As such, these examples contain no terms of self-appraisement, no personal evaluation, and no subjective assessment. The following are examples of fragments which contain self-appraisement, personal evaluation, or subjective assessment (all *italicized*) which you must *AVOID* using at all costs:

. Established *extremely successful* employment involvement program for 100-person manufacturing facility (don't say it's was "successful," show how it was).
. Created 100 ads *with impact* for six radio stations (instead demonstrate the "impact").
. *Creatively* designed large-scale technical training program for 350 computer assemblers (show what you did that was "creative").
. Researched offshore instrumentation *extensively* for

250-page technical operations manual (detail showing it was "extensive").

These words or phrases are not informative. They don't describe the problem you worked on, what you did, how you did it, or the results you achieved. Moreover, they tell your reader how you think they should evaluate your accomplishments. This can be both irritating and seen as arrogant whether you intend it that way or not. Put yourself in the reader's place. That can be a real turn off.

Instead, you need to just give the pertinent facts and let the reader make her or his own evaluations. After all, that's his or her role as decision maker for the position.

EXERCISE

Refinement of Your Functions

Go back to your functional inventory entries and amend your entries:

1. Make them sentence fragments.
2. Start each with a suitable action verb.
3. Give them lots of vivid, concrete, and necessary specific details.
4. Quantify them wherever possible.
5. Demonstrate their results.
6. Show your profit-consciousness by indicating bottom line impact.
7. Rework fragments to be sharper, cleaner, and shorter (10–20 words).

WHAT TO SEND OUT FIRST

Okay, you've made all your functional inventory entries represent as precisely and perfectly as possible your accomplishment of some significant activities you believe are relevant to that specific job opening for which you're applying. You need to determine the ten (10) best in general and for this job opening. However, be sure to keep *all* your functional inventory entries which may be useful for another opening.

"Now what?" you ask. "If these functional entries are *only* part of an inventory for creating what you're going to say when you present yourself, what are you actually going to give to the interviewer? They will definitely ask for your résumé. They *always* do. They'll undoubtedly ask for it even *before* the interview. So what will you actually provide to them?"

For the personnel department, interviewer, and decision maker, you will *ultimately* create a Job-Specific Résumé ... but not quite yet. You need to do something else first. Now that you have your functional inventory done, you're ready to get your job-getting self-promotion campaign under way. Your primary self-promotion vehicle will be what is called an "action letter."

WHAT'S AN ACTION LETTER?

This letter is an action-oriented promotional piece. This is based upon the ten fragments you created from the accomplishments you noted in your functional inventory (though you will *not* use all ten in the letter). It is a letter that you will send to decision makers in order to *line up interviews* for you. *Important Note*: The reason you send your action-letter credentials to potential employers is

NOT to get the job. Instead, it's to get the *interview*. Your interview is your opportunity to get your foot in the door so you can then create a positive, in-person, first impression and further promote yourself to the decision maker. The interview is where you learn *what the position is really about.* Face-to-face communication is essential for the decision maker to see you as part of the company team and a contributing employee.

TAILOR YOUR ACTION LETTER TO THE JOB

Everything in your action letter is targeted. That is, you tailor it to the company's perspective, based upon your research, as well as to the job's specifications. In your letter you show the decision maker that you are the one who has the experience and expertise:

1. In their specific business
2. With their specific product or service, or
3. In that specific type of work.

While some broader areas may be of interest to them as well, what they really want to see is an indication of your "goodness of fit":

1. You are experienced and productive.
2. You have the problem-solving experience that fits their wants, needs, and niche.
3. You have the performance results that fit their wants, needs, and niche.
4. You are a loyal, *team player*—"one of them" and "most of them."

Consider: Even if you send a brilliant, customized cover letter or an action letter <u>with the traditional résumé</u>, those who receive it will focus on the résumé. The cover letter, or the action letter looking like a cover letter, will tend to be thought of as a mere formality. As such, it carries no weight. It will likely be put aside, or deposited in the circular file, with the reader's attention directed at the résumé. Personnel departments are just like you. They've been instructed that the résumé is the thing of interest—the end-all and be-all—the ultimate position-matching document.

So the unfortunate reality is that too often a traditional résumé, irrespective of what accompanies it, can quickly and easily sabotage you. Such a scatter-shot document is likely to have little penetration and won't help the decision maker identify with you. In essence, you're throwing your credentials against the company's wall and hoping something will stick.

You need the first written contact with the decision maker to seize his or her attention, intrigue and hold her or his rapt attention because it is what is wanted. This is why whenever you can you will want to identify the job decision maker in the company and do research on this person as well. The decision maker is *the* individual you want to make the recipient of your action letter.

INTERACTING WITH PERSONNEL DEPARTMENTS

Most ads have the résumés go to the personnel department, also referred to as human resource departments. It is personnel departments that demand a résumé from you *before* they do anything with your application for the job—certainly before they will even consider giving you an appointment for an interview. Based only on your traditional résumé, personnel departments screen and eliminate candidates, weed out what they think are the real prospects from the warm bodies, and narrow the field of possibilities. This is because busy decision makers often don't have the time or inclination for this long, often-tedious process.

But while personnel departments will scan what you send and make recommendations to decisions makers, they are not, in general, the person for whom you would be working (unless, of course, you are seeking a human resources-related position). They are not the person who knows what *might* work in that particular job, even if what you say doesn't match the job specifications. Personnel staffers, especially in large companies, are usually handed a job specification sheet from which to work. As a result, in general they will likely have less latitude in going outside the specs the decision maker thought to write down in order to pick a candidate to schedule for an interview.

They may not see how uniquely your special qualities, skills, and experience fit the position. These critical discriminations are often something which only a decision maker who is working in that area may be much more likely to make. So whether you write an action letter or send a traditional résumé, if you go through the personnel department first or go only through them, you can short-circuit your ability and chances of reaching your real target audience, the decision maker for that position.

Consequently, your action letter needs to be

addressed to that specific job decision maker (without that traditional résumé) ... period. However, this approach is controversial and makes personnel departments and human resource people angry because it bypasses them and seems to discount their importance. They undoubtedly do their jobs professionally within the strictures of their own job descriptions within their companies but that doesn't mean they can necessarily be helpful to you. In my experience and that of others I assisted, the action letter directed at the decision maker works significantly better than going through the personnel department!

As I've said, while the action letter introduces you to the decision maker, it must grab the decision maker's attention. That is, it must also communicate your knowledge about the position as well as about the company's philosophy, goals, products, services, image, successes, solutions, and problems in its industry. It is about you only in reference to what you can do to enhance and benefit the company and help them accomplish their goals in the way *they want to do it*. Of course, at this point in time, you can't know precisely how *they* want to do it. That will come *through and after* your interview.

As a reminder, your action letter is geared to the company's foremost concern: "WIIFM" ("What's in it for me?") For the majority of businesses, they're not considering hiring someone in order for that person to have a job, take home a paycheck, buy a house, and raise a family. They are in business *only* to make a profit and survive in the marketplace.

ACTION LETTER AND RÉSUMÉ DIFFERENCES

Let me share a real-life example with you of how traditional résumés and action letters work differently in your job-getting campaign. Many years ago when I was looking for a job in organizational behavior consulting, I innocently followed the traditional résumé method. I sent out reams of résumés without a single success. Sure, I tailored my cover letter to the company and job, but the personnel departments focused on the résumé itself.

Unfortunately, my self-promotion pitch for the interview was in my cover letter which typically fell into a dark hole. With my cover letter seemingly overlooked or dismissed as just a formality, I was left without a way to promote myself. Consequently, when the personnel department looked at my traditional résumé's broad experience, I invariably received a form rejection letter.

Just then, Digital Equipment Corporation (DEC) placed an ad in the *Boston Sunday Globe* seeking an "organizational development consultant." I immediately researched the company and position (a little late in the process, but at least I *finally* did it!)

To my surprise I found not only the name of the person who would make the hiring decision, but also a discussion of an interesting problem an "OD specialist" would have to address in that particular job. I reworked and refined my functional inventory résumé then picked out the accomplishments that best related to the position. I used them for my performance-results and profit-oriented action letter to the decision maker. I made sure that everything I said reflected their company, department, position, goal, and their needs. Furthermore, I demonstrated how I had helped solve problems such as theirs, and indicated I wanted the opportunity to discuss with them my fit with their position.

The decision maker received *only* the action letter. No résumé, no cover letter. The personnel department received my traditional résumé with a cover letter. Ironically, just as I received the form rejection letter for my résumé from the DEC personnel department, I likewise received a personal letter from the decision maker who had set up an interview appointment for me. I got my foot in the door.

As you know all too well, nothing in the job-getting process is for sure. There is no 100%-guaranteed method for getting the job you want. But many who have tried the action-letter approach and compared it with the traditional résumé approach (whether to personnel departments or to decision makers) say they'll never send out a traditional résumé again ... period ... or even a customized résumé *until* they can tailor their résumé to the information they have gathered from their research AND, most specifically, the interview.

They've seen results of sending their action letter first, results that they had never seen with sending their traditional résumé. They were recognized. They got the opportunity of having an interview. They got to present and promote themselves to the decision maker in-person, not just on paper, to further make a good first impression. Never forget that a good first impression is like gold bullion: possessing permanent positive value.

WRITING AN ACTION LETTER

Once you have the name of the appropriate decision

maker, you can begin your letter. You want to write the first paragraph so that it's an attention-grabber. You need to highlight some interesting accomplishment that will make the employer want to read further.

For example, "As a marketing manager, I launched a new product which triggered first-year sales of $4 million in new China markets" or "As consultant to the president of the largest U.S. automotive parts manufacturer, I planned a productivity program for 10,000 employees saving millions of dollars in contracts." Of course, it doesn't have to be as grandiose as all that but it should be the show-stopper of all the successful things you have accomplished in your work that you can relate to the likely needs of the job opening. Keep in mind that even the most mundane accomplishment can be expressed interestingly.

You have to step back to see that what you've accomplished is both important and valuable. Sometimes we tend to dismiss and discount what we've accomplished and the successes we've had. Now is not the time for false modesty. You have to be willing to share your achievements with the decision maker without any undue humility. Decision makers really want to know what you have that they can *use*. So be as objective about what you've done as possible. You are simply stating facts. And remember: It's *not* about you. It's about what you've done that they want.

You need to let the decision maker know immediately that you're "seeking a more challenging and demanding position that will give you the opportunity to make substantive contributions" in your specialized area. Under no circumstances do you tell them you need a job or want more money. Even if they know it's the truth, they do not want to hear it. This is a game in which they want to be the object of your affection. They want you to drooling to work for them and be part of and a driver in their "glorious" future.

If you're currently employed, say so. If you're not, *don't* refer to it. Instead, you should simply refer to your experience, skills, and accomplishments and how they have been and *can be* beneficial.

Next you should present no more than five (5) qualifications in the form of bullets in your action letter. These are the action-oriented fragments we talked about. They start with the action verb and state your results-laden accomplishments that will be relevant to the company. These results must correspond as closely as possible to the stated required specifications listed in the ad. So when you respond to them, be sure you restate each job function this company desires, as stated in its ad, so the match you are making is obvious.

Next you write a paragraph detailing how you believe you'll fit in the job and organization. In it you demonstrate how you can make significant contributions in that area. This also helps show your knowledge about the company. They want to know you know all about them and so will fit in quickly and well. Finally, you indicate your most impressive, relevant educational background only.

You end your letter by *asking* (not begging) for an interview. You indicate you'll "be following up by telephone in five (5) working days." Later, after your follow-up call, if you haven't heard anything from the decision maker or company, you need to send a follow-up action letter in approximately five (5) weeks. Since your first presentation to potential employers is through your action letter, you must make it as *powerful and beneficial* as possible.

By the way, you say *nothing* in your action letter or final résumé that might suggest your age. In other words, you should not put down dates for anything in your past, such as you birth date, school years, or dates of various times of employment. You want to avoid any possible knee-jerk age discrimination especially if you're an older job applicant. You want them to focus on your experience in making profit-oriented actions and getting results that are right on target for them.

ACTION LETTER MODEL

The following is an example of an action letter:

Jonathan Brackett, Public Affairs Assistant
Associated Charities of New England
Re: Public Information Coordinator
Dear Mr. Brackett:

In a recent presentation to the Rotary Club on creating, projecting, and marketing business images, I demonstrated how their individual companies could increase their public favorability ratings as much as sevenfold in only one day. [*This was my intro to grab the reader's attention*]

As a communications professional, I have produced 197 published articles in national magazine and newspapers, media releases, 5 public service videos, newsletters, 5 non-fiction books, 15 seminars, a cable TV career-development program for 4 years, and corporate promotional flyers and brochures.

Since you are seeking a Public Information Coordinator to create public relations and promotional materials of all kinds in all media, you may be interested in my background. I have

. Created 25 articles, 53 PR releases, and 5 PSAs for the Charles River Unit of the American Cancer Society increasing public recognition of its services.

. Increased a new health-care service business's visibility state-wide by 66% via the print and electronic media and community events.

. Wrote 52 weekly articles on area business innovation and its relationship to social responsibility and assisting non-profits for a local paper.

. Designed layout and copy for 10,000-physician national direct-mail package for Fortune 500 pharmaceutical firm's surgical eye ointment.

. Originated 13 cable shows on PR to promote a marketing communications service, garnering 30 new clients in 3 months.

Holding a Ph.D. in Social Psychology from Boston University and M.Ed. in English, I have conducted research on the effects of interpersonal communication, presentation style, and image management on creating business visibility, credibility, and trustworthiness. I have presented the findings nationally.

My work with non-profit organizations, such as the American Red Cross headquarters and the American Cancer Society, has shown me that coordination of its public communications requires sensitivity, creativity, aggressiveness, and an intimate working knowledge of psychology and what media work best in what situations.

I will be glad to discuss my background with you in a personal interview. I'll call your office next week.

Sincerely,

ACTION LETTER'S IMAGE

But that's not all. You don't want your well-thought-out, carefully-constructed self-promotion piece (your action letter) to fall flat because of a cheap-looking presentation. You want the action letter you send to decision makers to scream *professionalism* and show your attention to quality and detail as well as your respect for them as its recipients.

This means you need to use high-quality, matching stationery for all letters to decision makers. Monarch-size paper (7" x 10") immediately differentiates your letter from other correspondence. If you do mass mailings of your action letter (without any résumé) to executive search firms or in response to ads' personnel departments, however, they may be on less expensive paper.

Moreover, research has indicated that colored paper tends to be better than white for gaining attention. But this doesn't mean just *any* color! Ivory, ecru, egg shell, off-white, pale gray are good because they are easy on the eyes and look professional. Others colors, especially bright colors, are likely to distract from your status and professionalism and look more like a flyer for a local garage sale.

However, a lot will depend upon the position for which you're applying and the personality of the company that has the position. In some cases, something unusual or with bright colors might be just the thing to get the decision maker to focus positively on you. You have to have a good sense of your audience and what's appropriate for them individually. That's why you learn all about them. But, generally speaking, it's always better to go for a more conservative approach—the same with your attire for your interview (as we'll discuss soon).

GOING FROM INVENTORY TO FINAL RÉSUMÉ

Yes, you will have to present a résumé at some point. But this will be your *job-specific résumé*. There are three (3) stages of résumé creation you need to go through: *functional inventory*, *customized general résumé*, and *job-specific résumé*. Your customized résumé employs all your functional activities that best represent you for the *type of work* you're seeking. This is slightly more general than the job-specific résumé because it's the boiler plate which you will tailor for each specific job opening.

FINAL RÉSUMÉ FORMAT

You need to construct your final company-customized résumé as a super-refined, job-specific, achievement-oriented functional document, something like the following format example:

Name
Address
Telephone number - home, *never* at work
Experience - generally how your experience matches the opening
Selected Experience - no more than five (5) past jobs in bullet form, stating what you accomplished for various companies or organizations with bottom line results (what you included in the bullets in your action letter). Include company/organization names and amount of time you were

with them but *leave out dates.*

Education - include *relevant* training, workshops, and seminars as well as formal schooling

Business/Professional Affiliations - *only* those organizations or associations that are relevant to the position, and *especially* where you have used your expertise to help them achieve their goals

References Upon Request - you want your references contacted *only* when the decision maker is serious about you for the job. You do not want them called by personnel as a matter of course. Check ahead of time on your references to make sure they will provide you with a positive evaluation. Not checking ahead of time can be lethal.

Your *job-specific résumé* should be *one page* and *one side only.* You should have it word-processed and printed on either a laser- or ink-jet printer so that looks crisp and professional. One and one-half-spaced lines are easier to read that single-spaced lines. It should have a lot of white space so what you write stands out and doesn't look crowded.

You need to keep in mind that ink, especially with laser printing that is not done professionally, can sometimes smudge on heavier, quality, and textured papers. If necessary, you can take your paper supply and final résumé original to the nearest copy place where they may be more likely to be able to control the possibility of ink smudging. First impression is all-important for documents that represent you too.

WHEN TO SUBMIT THE RÉSUMÉ

You want to forestall, as best you can, the inevitable of providing your résumé in any form to the decision maker and personnel department until you have gotten your interview. The interview will give you all kinds of job- and company relevant information and indications of good ways to relate to it and communicate it. Once you have this invaluable data, the résumé you finally send will be your post-interview, job-specific résumé.

However, I know you will likely be forced by the personnel department to submit a résumé *before* you have your interview. What you submit should be the most customized job-related résumé you can write, based on all your research to date. This will be one step removed from your final job-specific résumé which will be the result of your interview.

When the decision maker asks for your résumé, you can indicate that you'd like to give it to her or him later after you've learned from him or her about what the company wants for this particular position. In that way you can provide "precisely what she or he needs to know in order to see how you match their requirements." You can tell the decision maker that you'd like to mail or drop off a more "informed" résumé.

Once you have the interview, you will need to go over your not-quite-job-specific résumé to add anything especially relevant and memorable you learned about the company, job, and decision maker himself or herself during the interview. This would give you the opportunity to further polish your action letter and reiterate all the pertinent information you culled from the interview into your letter as well as the final submitted résumé. This finely tuned document then becomes your final, job-specific résumé which is given to the decision maker with a copy to the personnel department.

THINK OF YOUR RÉSUMÉ AS A BROCHURE

Your job-specific résumé will become the heart of your official record at the company. Even if the decision maker were to only scan it, you want to it to show you in the best light possible as the organization's best job match. You want it to emphasize your professionalism and focus on your competence. That's why it is important that you *not* include any personal information. Personal information can be distracting and, perhaps, biasing.

After your interview, you will write an *action cover letter* for your final job-specific résumé. In it you will express your appreciation for the interview (like a brief "thank you note") as well as reiterate your belief that you're the person for the job because of the specific and relevant job- and company information you have provided.

If there is something personal from the interview that you and the decision maker shared, you can include that because it can make you more personally identifiable and memorable. At the end of your cover letter you need to actually *ask for the job.*

Getting a job requires repetitive self-promotion with any one company. This is primarily because it takes about six (6) iterations of your job-matching qualifications to make you stand out in the decision maker's mind from the clamoring crowd of other applicants:

1. Your original action letter
2. If necessary, your *nearly* final customized résumé
3. Your interview
4. Your new, post-interview, job-specific résumé
5. Your "thank you" action cover letter, and
6. Your follow up call.

At any time but especially when times are tough economically, you need to think of yourself as a valuable commodity that the decision maker and company need and want. By promoting yourself as a significant benefit to them, you are *doing them a favor*. While you don't ever say this, you do demonstrate it by what you've done and your interest in their job and company.

By going out of your way to show how you match their desires, you are helping them solve their problem as soon as possible. Having a job opening costs them money. Your sequences professional behavior will demonstrate importantly both your knowledge and enthusiasm.

WHAT ABOUT REFERENCES

Your references should be individuals who know you and your work and are willing to speak positively about you. At the beginning of your job-getting campaign you need to discuss with them what you're going to emphasize and what you'd like them to stress when they're called about you. You need to discuss what you plan to say about them and let them blue-pencil it so it comes out the way they'd like. You need to give them a copy of your action letter and relevant sections from your customized and job-specific résumés to which to refer.

Some may want you to tell them what you'd like them

to say. In this situation, you can give them direction, guidance, and key words to use. But if they are uncomfortable about writing something to say, you can script their comments for them. However, you need to impress upon them that they need to speak in their own words so they will sound natural, sincere, un-coached, or unscripted.

It's also important for you to be prepared for a reference that goes bad. Hopefully you can avoid that by talking with your "references" ahead of time. If possible, talk with the potential reference in person. This way you can assess his or her body language or nonverbal cues, if the person seems comfortable and positive about doing it or on edge or irritated.

Sometimes people have negative feelings in general or about you particularly of which you're unaware. Sadly, sometimes the only way you may know something has gone awry, if the decision maker doesn't tell you directly, is if things seem strange after references have been contacted. In this event, you need to be sure to ask questions of the decision maker: Ask what happened— what went wrong. It's essential that you indicate that you'd like the opportunity to correct any incorrect or inaccurate impressions.

Once you know what happened, you need to explain the situation as best you can and then offer to provide another reference in its place. This is what happened to me. I was down to the wire for a research job. Everything had gone well until the employer talked to my references. After being treated like Mother Theresa, I was suddenly shunned like Typhoid Mary. When I asked the employer, he told me that while three of my references were glowing, one went for my jugular.

With a little coaxing, he told me what a former supervisor had said. I understood immediately what had happened. I objectively explained that just as the supervisor and I had begun to work together, he was badly burned by management because he had allowed another subordinate's research to be presented without being fully reviewed and critiqued by him ahead of time. After that, he seemed inordinately critical of everything any of his subordinates did. I stayed stay calm and non-judgmental about the situation and person. *Never bad mouth the person in any way.* With an explanation of the bad reference, the employer seemed more comfortable. I offered another reference in its place, one on which I knew I could count. I immediately deleted that "bad" reference from my list for the next job application.

In the future if you still *need* to use the "bad" reference, prepare the interviewer for it ahead of time. You do this by calmly and confidently explaining the circumstances under which you two worked together. However, you need to be understanding and stay non-judgmental. You should say *only* good things about that person in the process. You can suggest that as a consequence of this situation, the employer will likely receive a mixed or negative evaluation of you from this person. You can successfully counteract any negativity by:

. Detailing what that reference is likely to say and
. Providing each criticism with positive, results-oriented example of what you've accomplished that relates to the employer.

SUMMARY

In order to get the job you want in any economy, you need to know:

1. How to create a self-promotion plan for yourself.
2. How you can most productively approach those who make the real decisions on job openings
3. What your research has found to be an effective approach for you to use with each individual company
4. What your research has found to make you more likely to be seen as a good match for the job
5. How to transform your traditional résumé into a functional inventory
6. How to create on-point, targeted action letters
7. How to develop a bottom line- and results-oriented customized résumé
8. How to follow up with your final action letter and post-interview job-specific résumé.

Research has shown that this non-traditional promotional approach can make all the difference in your being successful in your job-getting campaign.

4

YOU'VE GOTTEN THE INTERVIEW APPOINTMENT: NOW WHAT?

How you handle yourself in a job interview can make or break you. Knowing how to present and promote yourself and ask and answer questions can help you eliminate the competition. According to Challenger, Gray, and Christmas, a Chicago-based global outplacement & career transitioning firm that leverages its expertise to create better opportunities, some 60% of job seekers don't get the offer they want simply because they fail to "sell" themselves.

Your job-getting campaign goal was first to get the interview appointment and you've accomplished that. Of course, like most job seekers you are probably still a little apprehensive. After all, you have a lot riding on getting through the interview unscathed and with flying colors. It's not just the job security and the money. It's also your self-esteem and fear of being a "failure."

But IF you're prepared, that is if you are:

. Coping with your anxiety
. Knowledgeable about the company and industry
. Matching what you've done with the job requirements
. Ready to show how you can uniquely benefit the company
. Showing how you positively and uniquely differ from the competition
. Ready with substantive questions to ask about the company and job
. Prepared to carry the conversational ball about 80% of the time
. Well-versed in how to present, promote, and "sell" yourself
… You will likely be a successful interviewee.

Notice I said "successful *interviewee*" and not a "successful job getter." No matter how brilliant your marketing campaign, how compelling your action letter, how successful your interview, and how job-specific your résumé is, you still may not get the job. While you can control most of the variables associated with you in your job hunt, you cannot control or guarantee the behavior of the other people involved.

You can't know their personal agendas, motivations, likes and dislikes, or possible hidden company agendas. You can't know if this position is really open to those outside the company or if it had to be posted as if it were open to outsiders but will automatically go to someone inside. What this means is that all you can do is present your best case and do it as persuasively as possible.

However, there are a few other things to be mindful of in an interview in order to give yourself a positive edge. Everything about you should focus on work performance and achievement. That means it's all about what you *do*, not who or what you are. Of course, you should be pleasant, upbeat, and positive with well-placed smiles, but mostly serious. Appropriate clothing and behaviors also matter.

WHAT TO WEAR

Don't let anyone tell you otherwise. Your attire in the interview is important. In fact, it's 90% of what people first notice when you walk in. What you wear suggests your goal for the upcoming interaction—either work or play. If your goal is work, your mode of dress should emphasize your skills, competence, experience, past successes, seriousness, and professionalism. But if it's a situation where your goal is play, you would dress to emphasize fun (to whatever degree is appropriate). Or if your goal is attractiveness, your dress would emphasize your body and beauty attributes.

Your clothes need to reflect this. The conventional wisdom is that no matter how laid-back a company may be in its day-to-day business, where jeans and running shoes are the uniform, you need to go to the interview dressed formally. Leave your casual dress at home for when you get the job.

CONVENTIONAL INTERVIEW GARB

This conventional job-interview wisdom suggests business suits for both men and women. For women an alternative to the suit can be a jacketed dress or skirt, blouse, and jacket. But the jacket is a *must* because it suggests power and seriousness.

Interestingly, in psychological experiments when people compared pictures of a woman wearing a sweater, skirt, and blouse and the same woman wearing a jacket and the same skirt and blouse, they thought the woman wearing the sweater looked like a secretary and the woman in the jacket looked like a manager.

For men an alternative to a suit may be a sports coat and slacks. This will depend upon the conservativeness of the company. IBM and the FBI, for example, tend to require a very specific appearance. However, even with the more casual sport coat and slacks, a tie is a must. Research has shown that wearing a tie is associated with power and professionalism.

At one time slacks were considered *verboten* for women at work. Fortunately that is changing. However, not every company finds them acceptable. But where they are, it's imperative that they are of natural materials, subdued colors, well-tailored, fit properly, and are *not* form-fitting or body hugging. Anything that adds a note of attractiveness or sexuality detracts from the goal of being taken seriously. Women still have that gender-stereotyped burden of tending to be looked at as a sexual object rather than as a serious business professional.

Even with casual slacks, a jacket of some kind continues to be necessary. Depending upon the company's philosophical preferences, there may be a desire that the jacket be the same color as the slacks, rather than a complementary or contrasting color.

Since women still tend to be judged more stringently

in business, her shoes should also look more business-like than appealing. For example, closed toes and low-to-moderate heels suggest seriousness. Open-toed shoes and high heels suggest attractiveness and sexuality. Keep in mind that high- or spike heels make the leg more obvious and make the derriere much more prominent.

The same goes for other physical and superficial features: hair length, for example. Shoulder-length hair worn down is still business-like, whereas long flowing hair bespeaks of casual fun and sexuality. Jewelry and makeup need to be appropriate and minimal, depending upon the company and job.

This goes for facial piercings. If you have them, remove them. They tend to be seen as too avant-garde. As I said, what they allow on the job and what they expect in an interview may be two entirely different things. Keep in mind that you don't want to do anything that smacks of theatricality unless that's the ambiance in which you're going to be working. But, even then … it all depends.

DETERMINING YOUR ATTIRE

To avoid embarrassment it's very useful to try to find out ahead of time what the typical "costume" of the job decision maker is. Whenever possible you want to emulate the tone, style, and look. Why? This is because you want to appear to be "one of them." If they can visualize you as blending in with the company, you'll more likely be seen as fitting in. If you can't find out about the specific decision maker, at least get an idea how management at that level of the company dresses or how workers in general dress. All you need is a clue then dress a bit more conservatively than that.

OVER-FIFTY INTERVIEWS

If you're 50 or over, you will tend to automatically have a strike against you. People who are older tend to have a great deal more experience and, thus, will need to be paid more for it. Younger, less experienced people will work for less and are easier to come by as replacements. And when there is a merger or economic downturn, it is often the older members of the company who are let go.

However, there are things you can do to give you an edge. You need to do everything you can to give the impression of vibrant health and a high energy level. Today age 50 is not "old." In fact, it's more like yesterday's 35. It's really prime time! You need to think of this when preparing and meeting the interviewer then:

1. Shake hands firmly.
2. Speak clearly and concisely.
3. Give your brief "I want the job" introduction with tempered enthusiasm.
4. Maintain good eye contact.

Everything you do should shout that you have a positive *can-do* attitude as well as the abilities and background to support it. Both men and women should look contemporary and solid but not faddish. Your hairstyles, clothing, makeup, and accessories—your whole appearance— should be that of a person ten years your junior—but *not* younger. There's something perceived to be pathetic about a person 50 or older trying to look like a 20- or 30-something.

You need to wear your experience and accomplishments like a badge of honor. You worked hard to get where you are and what you are. And, by golly, you are not apologizing for it! As I mentioned, make your attire business-like, conservative, but up-to-date and middle-age appropriate. For men know what tie widths are in. The same goes for jacket lapels, trouser leg widths, and whether this is the era of the cuffed or cuff-less trouser.

If you knew your interviewer were male and went to a particular school that you likewise attended and that he preferred to wear his school tie, you'd want to have on the same tie whenever possible for mutual identification. If you knew anything else about what the person would likely be wearing, male or female, for your interview, you'd want to have on something similar if possible because similarity fosters attraction.

For women, you need to wear what would be appropriate for business only. Don't wear any fabrics, styles, accessories, or footwear that have an age-association—either too old or too young. Natural-looking makeup that highlights your best features is good. It shouldn't stand out but make you look vibrant and healthy. Moreover, you need to watch out for strong contrasts, like too bright or dark lipstick, too harsh blush, eyeliner, eyebrow pencil line, or shadow. Keep in mind that too much makeup doesn't cover up age. It accentuates and draws attention to it. Less is definitely more.

Since how we look substantially determines how others see us, this concern is not frivolous. Looking older detracts from your knowledge, expertise, skills, experience, success, and vibrancy ... and may even overshadow them because of age bias and possible discrimination.

If you believe that certain physical facial features, such as bags, drooping eye folds, sagging throat, and deep character lines are detrimental to your job-getting campaign, you may consider cosmetic surgery or cosmeceuticals. This is true for both women and men who are increasingly taking advantage of cosmetic surgery and less invasive anti-aging serums, chemical fillers, line minimizers, and more.

If you choose to consider cosmetic assistance, you need to look for physicians who are certified by the American Academy of Facial and Reconstructive Surgery. If you're unsure about a professional's qualifications, you can call the State Board of Registration in Medicine in your state. Most cosmetic surgeons offer a free consultation to evaluate you and your desires and suggest options.

You want to ask the cosmetic surgeon for references and see examples of before and after photos of her or his work. There are many minor and extensive procedures that can enhance your physical presentation of yourself, from chemical facial peels to filling in facial creases to full facelifts, with lots of procedures along a continuum in between. However, if you go this route, you should know that there are risks, especially with any surgery. As a consequence, consider seriously what you want to accomplish and don't take these risks lightly.

In sum, if you are 50 or over, that is a fact. But that doesn't mean you have to advertise it. It doesn't mean you have to accept a negative assessment of it either.

What you'll want to impress the interviewer with is that you represent loyalty, maturity, flexibility, job savviness, productivity, and the "old-fashioned" work ethic. Without referring to it specifically, you need to show that your age is actually a real benefit for the company. You are NOT "old," but "wise, seasoned, experienced, results- and profit-oriented." Furthermore, as such, you don't need expensive and extensive training before you'll be productive and contributing to their bottom line. This can save them big bucks.

YOUR ENTRANCE

You will be viewed and treated the way you present yourself and the way you demonstrate you expect to be treated. First and foremost, be punctual. It's rude to be late. It's also awkward to be early because it may put pressure on the interviewer to hurry up whatever he or she is doing to meet with you. That can create guilt which doesn't enhance her or his first impression of you.

When you enter the interviewer's office, present yourself with assurance and assertiveness. That means what some have called "military bearing." You want to stand tall, with your shoulders back, stomach pulled in, and head held high. This immediately makes you look confident with high self-esteem. Slouching which tends to make your head droop and your body fall into itself. This makes you look, perhaps, as if you don't respect yourself and have low self-esteem. Not a good first impression no matter how brilliant, expert, or experienced you are.

If you're announced and expected, do not knock. That behavior suggests timidity. Instead, just walk in confidently and directly. Hopefully as you enter, the interviewer will rise to greet you and shake hands. Even if the interviewer doesn't extend his or her hand to you, extend yours to him or her. If the interviewer is seated behind a desk, walk to the side of it so you shake hands firmly, and pull the interviewer toward you ever so slightly. You should consider holding the grip just a heartbeat longer than the interviewer does. Doing so can enhance the perception of your confidence, control, and rapport. If you're smiling sincerely as you do so, it is less likely to make a negative impression or be seen as aggression.

WHERE TO SIT

Immediately look for a chair to sit down. You should sit *after* the interviewer sits or when the interviewer motions for you to sit. *If* you have the option, pick a chair at the side of the desk which would, in effect, equalize the power differential between you and the interviewer. If not, it may be better not to consider even *casually asking* if you can move a chair a short distance to the side which would eliminate having the interviewer's desk between you.

You need to keep in mind that the job applicant's chair has likely to been strategically placed in front to maintain the perception of authority. The desk which is a symbol of power acts as a barrier between you two. This arrangement automatically makes the interviewer one-up, and you one-down. Being aware of this ahead of time allows you to know what to expect, be prepared, and reduce your anxiety and feelings of potential intimidation.

BE YOURSELF BUT MODERATE

While you want to show initiative and confidence, you need to be careful not to come on too strong. Being too dynamic, intelligent, or positive can intimidate or turn off an interviewer. I encountered this when going for an interview for a clinical internship. I was very upbeat and positive and this, unfortunately, was interpreted as a lack of flexibility. My sponsor was amazed when they turned me down because she knew I was anything but "inflexible."

Being perceived as acting as though you know *everything* about the job and company immediately creates a bad impression. You need to show that you are aware of the job, company, and industry but that interviewer knows more about them than you do. You want to appear smart but also deferential to this person's "superior knowledge" on the subject. This is particularly true if the interviewer is not the final decision maker which is sometimes the case. Showing this kind of respect makes you more likable. Never forget that likability is important irrespective of your job qualifications. The more likable you are, the more similar you appear to be.

While in the office, you need to observe everything you can. You want to make mental note of anything to which you can relate, such as photos, books, plaques, objects denoting interests, hobbies, education, affiliations, etc. If it seems appropriate, you'll want to be able to make comments and ask questions about the interviewer as a person and show interest and what you have in common. "I see by your photo you play golf. Golf is one of my favorite activities. I'm still learning. Are there 18-hole golf courses in the area where you play?" While this questioning is somewhat personal, you can keep it casual and somewhat neutral. Doing so can create mutual interest and foster a positive in-person first impression of you.

You want to establish a rapport with the decision maker and hopefully develop some identification with you. Commonality creates a bond. Similarity breeds identification, attraction, and liking. You want the interviewer to feel comfortable with you as a person too, not just a job candidate.

INTERVIEWS: DOS AND DON'TS

There are definitely things that you should and should not do during interviews:

Don't drink. If the interview is conducted in a restaurant instead of the office, you should *not* drink anything alcoholic. Even if your interviewer "drinks lunch," you must not join in. Having a drink can reflect on you negatively.

The person may be testing you to see you are a "three-martini-lunch-er." When you don't succumb, you may be in a better bargaining position. Moreover, your thought processes will be clearer and you can stay more focused on what you need to communicate as well as how the interviewer is responding to it. The same goes for an alcoholic drink in the office. No matter how cozy the chat or how chummy the interviewer seems to get, you need to resist the impulse.

Research has shown that people tend to be in better spirits in an environment of eating and drinking (though not necessarily alcohol). This means the interviewer at lunch might be more persuadable in her or his decision making. Of course, it's important to remember that being influenced can go both ways—you, too, are more likely to be influenced in that situation as a result.

Don't smoke. Despite the fact that approximately one-quarter of Americans still smoke, smoking especially in business environments has become generally unacceptable. Lighting up in the interviewer's office is seen negatively for a number of reasons. It suggests nervousness, that you need the nicotine to relax you. It fills the air with smoke, the room and perhaps your clothing with ash, and covers you with the smoke odor. Even if the interviewer lights up, you must not do it.

What can you do if the interviewer lights up and tobacco smoke affects you negatively (as it does me)? You can pleasantly request the interviewer not smoke in your presence. Of course, it's better to say something *before* he or she actually lights up and the smoke starts to billow. Many people hate grinding out an unfinished cigarette. So the moment you see the cigarette appear, make your request.

If the interviewer shows dislike of your request about not smoking, you need to immediately ask yourself what this means with respect to how employees are treated in the organization. It also should bring up questions about whether there are any restrictions on smoking and keeping an unpolluted work environment. An unpolluted environment is not only better for your health but also better for your productivity.

Don't chew gum. If your mouth is dry, suck inconspicuously on a cough drop or a breath mint. Chewing is not only distracting to watch but also noisy.

It's perceived as a nervous habit. It's also seen as un-business-like and a too-informal thing to do.

Don't name drop. Attempting to impress the interviewer by introducing names of well-known people of your acquaintance tends to sound phony, arrogant, and superficial. It also tends to sound as if you fear you can't sell yourself on your own merits alone so you're relying on your associates to take up the slack. It's as if the power of status of those "celebrities" will rub off on you by your association with them. While research on social power suggests that it does in general, it's not the case in this situation.

I experienced this first-hand. Sadly I had no idea that my mentioning someone of note would be misperceived as "name-dropping." I was interviewing with a group (watch out for *group* interviews!) at a college for a position of curriculum developer. At one point in the conversation, I mentioned Dr. Robert Chin, internationally-known organizational development consultant. Immediately, one interviewer announced she thought it was inappropriate for me to "name-drop."

I was aghast. Dr. Chin was my doctoral dissertation advisor. He and I had worked closely for some time. In response to my request for a referral, he told me he would send a letter on to them before my interview to acquaint them with me. I mentioned him to jog their memories and be able to discuss what we had been doing together and how it might relate to the job at hand.

Oops! On the contrary, they hadn't received it. And my explanation—which came too late— fell on deaf, disbelieving ears. They'd already made up their minds about this "name-dropper." I had innocently poisoned the well. However, when you're asked about your experience with a particular "name," you can then talk about it matter-of-factly and briefly. Specifically you should emphasize what you and the other did together and what you achieved as a result. The rule of thumb with "names" is if you're in doubt, don't mention them.

Don't get into an argument. You can't avoid disagreement, but you can avoid an argument. Being *assertive*—standing up for yourself but doing so calmly and respectfully—is important when you need to express that disagreement. It's the same for using *active listening* methods—using "I-messages," speaking in terms of how *you* see things, how *you* feel about them, and what *you'd* like to see done. I-messages do not argue with, judge the other, or criticize him or her. They only give your personal perspective on an issue. Using these two inter-related approaches, you can effectively control your emotions, reduce anger in the other person, and guide the direction and intensity of the interaction.

If the interviewer disagrees with your point of view or method of having done something, you should "agree that there *may* be a number of reasonable approaches to take to address the problem." Then you should re-state that "you're pleased the one you used produced the desired result in that particular situation." People disagree for many reasons besides simply holding a different point of view. They may be trying to show you they know what you're talking about. They may be trying to demonstrate superiority. Or, they may be testing you by trying to see how confident, flexible, or easily stressed you are in your thinking and approach.

Don't tell jokes. Humor can be a very touchy area.

What is humorous to one person may be offensive or just plain stupid to another. Jokes are especially hazardous since they often involve laughing at other people. Moreover, joking is inconsistent with the image of seriousness you want to convey. However, this doesn't mean you should err in the other direction either. If you're too serious and formal, the interviewer might see you as rigid and wonder how well you would get along with others. Fortunately there is a middle ground.

Very mild, self-deprecating humor can lighten the interview. By making yourself the brunt of a joke or showing that you're innocuously fallible, you can, in fact, make yourself more likable. If you have a flair for telling short, relevant anecdotes about yourself, you may consider interjecting some humor at a few appropriate points, preferably toward the end of the interview.

Whatever you do, don't over-do the self-deprecating humor. Repeated mentions of fallibility, however mild, might be misconstrued as lack of confidence or low self-esteem. Also, if you don't easily relate things humorously, you should not use the interview as the time in which you'll give it a try. Instead, as the interview comes to a close, you can simply relax and smile more.

Don't fidget. There are numerous unconscious behaviors which signal discomfort or anxiety. You need to avoid all excessive body movement, such as:

. Wringing your hands
. Clenching your fists
. Gripping chair arms
. Tapping your toes
. Drumming your fingers

. Cracking your knuckles

. Jiggling your foot or knee

. Scratching or rubbing yourself

. Playing with an object, such as pen or papers

. Chewing your hands, nails, pen, or eyeglass earpieces

. Crossing and uncrossing your legs or arms

. Twirling your hair

. Fingering objects or clothing

. Bobbing your head in constant agreement

. Pacing

. Slouching

. Leaning back in your chair too comfortably and casually

. Avoiding eye contact

. Yawning

. Sighing

. Sniffling

. Lip smacking

. Licking lips

. Covering your mouth with your hand in any way

. Rocking the chair

. Shifting your position

. Biting your lower lip

. Resting your chin on your hand

. Playing with your cell phone—keep it turned off, period!

. Clicking your pen

. Touching various parts of your body

. Smiling too much—makes you look submissive, wanting approval.

WHAT IMPACTS THE INTERVIEWER'S MEMORY

There are two memory effects that you need to remember. One is the *primacy effect*. This suggests that whatever you do *first* will be well-remembered because it has created a first impression, which can be like a large, sparkling, multi-faceted diamond. The other is the *recency effect*, which suggests that whatever you do *last* will be well-remembered because it's the interviewer's most recent recollection of you.

Both come into play in the interview situation. As a result, you need to actively create both a positive first impression and a positive last impression. You want to tweak their interest, entice them, and attract them to identify with you. This is something you need to plan for well in advance of your interview. While you are expected to be alert, positive yet serious throughout your entire interview, what you say and do at the beginning and end act as bookends for your total in-person presentation.

"TELL ME ABOUT YOURSELF"

Before you do anything else, you want to start off with a "This is why I want the job" statement. You would briefly indicate that based on your research of the company within the industry that you feel the position:

1. Fits with your career plans and values
2. Is where you believe you can learn, grow, and develop
3. Is where you can make your greatest, most productive contribution.

Since about 80% of job interviews start with "Tell me about yourself," you need to be completely prepared and ready with a brief statement in story form, using references to your knowledge of the company. This will help create rapport and identification. It will help make the interviewer on a subconscious level see you as "one of us." This will require you to "sell" yourself.

SELL YOURSELF IN 30-SECONDS

Ready. Set. Go! You have up to 30 seconds.
. Just 30 seconds to "Tell me about yourself"
. Just 30 seconds to grab and hold your listener's attention
. Just 30 seconds to make your point
. Just 30 seconds to convince and persuade
. Just 30 seconds to create your first impression as a job applicant effectively.

Why only 30 seconds? Because 20-30 seconds is the TV-generation's attention span. We expect everything to be short. Short has impact. That is why we tend to think and speak in sound bites. They're easy to digest, absorb, and remember. Moreover, business people, especially interviewers, have busy schedules and are impatient to get to the heart of the matter. They have things they want to know and then go on to the next item on their list. They don't want to wait ten minutes for you to get around to the point you want to make. Besides you'll lose them quickly along the way if you are not brief and to the point.

If you spend your 30 seconds wisely and have gotten the interviewer's attention, you will have up to another 3–4 minutes to follow up with your core message. This means you need to decide on your 30-second story strategy in advance. If you're going to grab attention, make a positive impression, and sell your message, you need to know:

1. What image you want to project
2. What your communication goals are
3. Who your target audience is
4. How you're going to accomplish your goal by covering the *who, what, where, why,* and *how* of it.

HOW RON USED HIS 30 SECONDS

For example, Ron M. is an international political journalist interviewing at *Newsweek*. To date he's been a freelancer contributing articles to all the big-name magazines and newspapers but now he wants something which is steadier where he can expand his experience and further develop his political writing talents. Here's what he says initially about himself and his job goal:

"I've noticed that *Newsweek*'s foreign reporting covers the Middle East less than other areas. People are clamoring for more information. I believe this gap needs to be filled. For the past 15 years I've covered the Middle East, writing articles on it for *New York Times*, *New Yorker*, and *Vanity Fair*, for example. My five-part series on Afghanistan's struggling economy in *Harpers* has been nominated for a Pulitzer My experience in the Middle East may help fill that gap, further contributing to your magazine's international readership."

For your job interview, you should prepare your 30-second selling point with seven self-promotional techniques in mind:

1. *State Your Objective*. What do you want to achieve through the interview? Information? A referral? A job? You have to know precisely what you want so you can ask the right questions. (Ron wants to be on the writing staff of *Newsweek*.)

2. *Know Your Audience*. Who is your audience? (Ron's audience is an upper-level editor at a magazine.) Is this person a decision maker? (Yes.) What does the person want in return? (An excellent writer to improve their inadequate Middle East coverage.) What are the interests of the decision maker? (To add further quality to the magazine to increase readership and profits.) What's important? (Knowing that Ron has received praise from his peers and respect for his ability and extensive experience.)

3. *Listen*. Half of communication is listening. You must listen carefully so you can correctly interpret and understand what the other person says so you can correctly apply it to your presentation.

4. *Use the Right Approach*. What single, direct sentence best leads to your objective? (For Ron, "I've noticed that *Newsweek*'s foreign reporting covers the Middle East less than other areas. People are clamoring for this information.") What builds a case around your statement? ("For the past 15 years I've covered the Middle East, writing articles on it for *New York Times*, *New Yorker*, and *Vanity Fair*, for example.")

You need to find common ground on which to relate your statement to the needs, interests, and experience of your listener. ("My five-part series on Afghanistan's economy in *Harpers* has been nominated for a Pulitzer"). He knows there are many distinguished Pulitzer Prize-winning writers on Newsweek's staff.

5. _Use a Hook_. Whether you're promoting yourself, a product, service, or course of action, you need to get your listener's attention—with a hook. Finding a hook means looking for something unusual, exciting, dramatic, humorous, or personal about your subject. In the case of the interview, the subject is "you." (Ron's hook was there was a "reporting gap" and "people were clamoring for the information" which he could provide.)

Questions, instead of statements, are also often effective. (Ron could ask, "What are people clamoring for that _Newsweek_ isn't yet providing fully?" and then provide his own answer, "Greater coverage of the Middle East political scene.") Whatever your hook is, it must relate to both your objective and your listener, as well as lead to the point you want to get across.

6. _Offer Supporting Material_. Every point you make needs support, documentation, and amplification to give it weight and clarification. The more personal or visual the support the better. Facts, figures, examples, testimony, anecdotes, imagery, and visual aids give a point substance, vividness, and life. You want to relate to both _reason_ and _emotion_.

7. _Ask For What You Want_. What do you want from your listener? How do you want them to respond to you? Do you want an action or reaction? If you want an action, then you need to ask to have a specific action performed within a specific time frame. (Ron might say to Newsweek's editor, "Give me a list of any other documents you want and I'll send them to you by courier.") If you want a reaction, you should use the power of suggestion. (Ron might say, "What I need is

someone who likewise sees the importance of reporting on the Middle East.")

T-BAR VIGNETTES

Because the interviewer will ask you for more detail about particular functions you list in your introductory statement and on your action letter that are of interest to the company, you should have a scenario or anecdote in mind for each bulleted function. These will briefly tell an on-point story or scenario. To construct them you need to:

1. Tell the situation or problem on which you acted
2. Proceed into what you did
3. Tell the results you got
4. Show the bottom-line effects of what you did.

An easy way to construct and remember your important functions' descriptive scenarios or anecdotes is through T-BAR vignettes. T-BAR is an acronym for Topic sentence, Background, Action, and Results.

For example, suppose the interviewer asks if you are creative. You are and want to emphasize your ability to be creative. But you do not want to say, "Yes, I'm creative." That's totally uninformative because it doesn't tell what you've done. It doesn't relate your achievements to the company's bottom line. What you need to do instead is present a vignette in which you *demonstrate* your creativity using T-BAR:

1. *Topic Sentence*: "I've done a number of things I believe demonstrate my creativity."

2. _Background_: "One example is when I worked on an automobile advertising campaign. The company's promotional material was to increase the product's market share, but it failed."

3. _Action_: "I researched the car's market, ran focus groups, and discovered that half of the market wasn't buying the product because the product ads didn't appeal to their thinking style. So I developed ads which presented the car graphically for those who respond emotionally and verbally for those who respond intellectually."

4. _Results_: "Within six months sales increased 18% and the market share gained five share points."

EXERCISE
Constructing Accomplishment Vignettes

1. Think of 10 strengths you want to stress in an interview.

2. Construct a vignette for each strength using the T-BAR example above.

3. Once you have these vignettes ready, rehearse them so that you know them so well they will just roll off your tongue when you want to share them.

4. Practice! Practice! Practice!

5. The more comfortably and confidently you present them, the more impact they'll have.

6. The more comfortably and confidently you present them, the more persuasive you will be as a results-oriented achiever.

PREPARE QUESTIONS IN ADVANCE

Your interviewer wants to see that you are interested in delving into the company and all that relates to the job you're seeking. If you don't ask questions, you may be seen as uninterested in the job or not as interested in them as they are in you. Even if you decide in the interview that the job isn't for you, you need to continue to do everything you should *as if* you were.

Remember: Decision makers in different companies talk. If one mentioned you had an appointment coming up and the other had already seen you, you'd want the second interviewer to receive a positive report on your interest, background, and how you conducted yourself. Knowing that you'd already been seen by the first company and were evaluated positively, the second company might be even more eager to interview you. It helps create a positive first impression. In one sense, *when you prepare for one interview, you prepare for all of them.*

So you never want to be caught flat-footed, unprepared by not having and asking relevant questions about the job and company. This means it's always a good idea to create a large list of questions that you prepare to ask the interviewer.

The following are a few *essential* ones to include. Keep in mind that the company has problems to solve and the more they can tell you about those problems, the better you can demonstrate your ability to help them solve them—to relieve their "pain." Be sure to show you have done your homework when it comes to having researched and understanding the company. Be sure to include references to what you have learned and where. Depending upon what your research has revealed and what the interviewer shares with you, you may not need to ask all these questions:

. What do you feel are your highest-priority projects for the remainder of this year?

. What do you see as your biggest problem currently in ___? (expand to show you have some knowledge of a problem area they have had)

. How do you see the person in this position helping your department succeed in meeting its goals?

. What are the scope and details of the job?

. What are the areas of responsibility (performance factors)?

. What specific skills and/or experiences would help someone do well in this job?

. What are their expectations for you in the first 90 days, six months and a year?

. To whom would you report?

. With what kind of people would you be working?

. What is the growth potential? (What are the possibilities for promotion?)

. What is the philosophy of the organization? (Hopefully you will already have ascertained this, but it's not always easy to ascertain.)

. Why is there currently an opening? (If possible get the name of the last person in the job—getting their perspective on the job and why they are leaving could be useful.)

. If the person previously holding the job was promoted, how long were they in the job before their promotion?

. Will you have a chance to meet co-workers before you accept the position?

. When is the first job performance evaluation done?

. Does the company anticipate changing its current

structure anytime soon? (If anything is in the works about downsizing or merger, hopefully this will have been in the general or business news so you should have picked this up already.)
. What is the timeframe for/availability of this position? (this week, a month, six months?)

INTERVIEW SELLING STYLES
Job interviews are an exercise in both marketing and "selling." How you sell (promote and close) is as important as what you sell. Presenting yourself, handling questions, showing knowledge about the general area, the job, and the company, and later, negotiating, rely on the calculated "sales" strategies. These strategies include listening, observing, responding to nuances of the situation, and adapting your tempo and style to the situation and your goal.

While no two selling/self-promoting situations are the same, there are approaches you can adapt and apply. The approach you use depends mostly upon you and how comfortable you are with being assertive. But it also relates to how the company operates and expects its employees to operate.

While assertiveness is good, aggressiveness tends to be over the top. You decide to adopt whatever seems useful and appropriate to the circumstances, which means you don't have to stick to one style if it doesn't seem to be working or applicable.

Hard Sell. This old-style approach dictated that any kind of self-promotion/selling relentlessly should hammer away at the person you were trying to convince to buy your services. This covered what you did, for whom, and how you were to achieve your results.

In an interview you would inundate the interviewer with facts about your accomplishments, overwhelm them with your energy, zeal, and commitment. You would communicate a sense of pressure and hurriedness. In effect, you would be demanding the job because you knew you deserved it.

Warning: While this approach *may* work on old-time, cynical, and skeptical interviewers, particularly in a sales-related area, it doesn't work well with others, particularly in today's marketplace. One big reason is that it focuses on what *you* want and *not* on what the company wants.

Also, for a female to use this approach it is especially risky. Many people, but males particularly, still expect the more subdued behavior of the female stereotype. This suggests that if your behavior is too far removed from their expectations, it could cost you the job.

<u>*Soft Sell*</u>. This is the newer, more acceptable style for both men and women. It is subtly assertive. In general, while you appear to be letting the employer take the initiative, you are quietly and carefully guiding the action. Rather than relentlessly barraging the interviewer with accomplishment after accomplishment, you psych out the person. In a "go-with-the-flow," unhurried style you play the political game. That is, you tell them what they want to hear but without the overwhelming, in-your-face pressure. What you're promoting/selling is your personality as strong, reasonable, and flexible as well as your productivity and the results you have accomplished. You arc direct and you keep showing how your experience and expertise match the job but you are

a bit more low-key about it.

You gently remind the interviewer of what the matches are between the job specs and you. You further demonstrate how there is a similarity between your experience, the job, and the company's ideology and goals. In an almost effortless way you make company-relevant remarks (such as something you read about their new product) and offer similar bottom-line-oriented achievements. All the while, you appear confident, pleasant, and helpful. But most importantly, you show you are focusing on *what best helps the company achieve its goals*—not what helps you achieve your goals.

Remember: As I've mentioned, the employer is always looking at "what's in it for me." They really don't care what you want to get out of it as long as the match gets them what they want. There's rarely anything warm and fuzzy about their desires in this context.

This approach is based on my personal marketing seminars and programs. What I have found is that you can significantly influence the decision maker in any situation (interviewer, customer, or client) in your favor if you provide useful, valuable information and benefits while developing a trusting and identifying relationship.

EXERCISE
Your "Sales" Skills Assessment

How good are your marketing and "sales" skills? Can you get peoples' attention? Can you persuade them to take what you're giving: your ideas, skills, expertise, and experience? Can you demonstrate how you provide value that they need?

Rate your sales skills from 1-10 with 8-10 = very good to excellent; 5-7 = fair to good; and 1-4 = needs improvement.

__I know precisely what I have to offer.

__I know how it compares to the competition.

__I know how to tailor my achievements to the employer's needs.

__I have researched necessary information on the company.

__I can write an action letter to get the employer to see me.

__I can confidently meet the interviewer, answer questions, and ask relevant questions.

__I can state my case assertively and persuasively.

__I can focus on what the company wants.

__I can appeal to their wants showing my benefits and value.

__I can ask for what I want, even offering, *if necessary*, to work for them without pay for a month to demonstrate how I can help them.

For your final score, add the ratings and divide by 10.

MONEY: WHO ASKS FIRST

Money is always a difficult subject. In general, you should *not* be the one to introduce the subject. Your concern is supposed to be the company and what you can do for them. (They know you want the job for you; you know you want the job for you; but you both play the game.) To bring up the subject of money, especially early in the decision-making process, is seen as uninformed, unprofessional, overly eager, and, perhaps, desperate.

If the interviewer asks you how much you want to make, do NOT respond directly. Instead, answer indirectly. Why? Your answer should, once again, indicate that you're "*more* interested in the *challenge of the job* and *what you can do for the company* than its monetary rewards." When you answer, you indicate that "your salary requirements will depend upon:

. How your potential is realized and

. What responsibilities you have."

You should already have some sense of what the pay scale is and know how this measures up to the average for your region and the industry. Once the interviewer introduces the topic, however, you can inquire about the *salary range of the position.* Assuming your desired salary and what is offered aren't too disparate, you can casually indicate that "you believe there's room for discussion." Period.

It's very helpful, as part of your job-getting research, to look at the industry's salary range of the position (1) below the one you want then look at the range for the position (2) above, specifically: *The high end of the range for the position below what you're seeking ($5,000 below) and the low end of the position above ($10,000 above) what you're seeking should give you a ballpark figure.*

Put another way, you should aim for a 20% increase in salary over your last position. That is assuming that your last salary was on par with the industry and regional average. Of course, the overall economic condition at the time can influence what you seek for a salary ... as well as what they'll be willing to pay. This increases the number of choices you have, gives you flexibility, and provides some latitude in negotiating for what you want when you're offered the job.

Just to obtain a job in difficult times may require that you rethink the salary for which you ask. Showing that you can be flexible and that the company's welfare is your *real* focus can improve your chances. A good performer who always does more than is required is more likely to get closer to what she or he wants when the economy or the company's financial situation improves.

If you don't gather salary information prior to the interview, you will be doing yourself a real disservice. You may accept a figure that too low or you may price yourself out of the competition. Information is power! The better informed you are the better able you'll be to control your salary negotiation.

Since salaries are generally assigned to positions but may be assigned to individuals, you have some flexibility, depending upon the company's perception of your productivity and performance. Therefore, you need to establish your value in the eyes of the decision maker.

It's important to remember that interviewer's perceptions will also vary based on personal things, such as beliefs or degree of personal identification with the job applicant. What this suggests is that even if two individuals present precisely the same skills and work experience, one may be favored over the other for subjective reasons over which you have no knowledge or control.

As a consequence, you want to do what you can to help this interviewer come to know, like, and trust you. You want to do what you can to help this person come to perceive you as valuable as both a person and as a contributor to the team and the company. Your multi-faceted perceived value will be the foundation upon which you will negotiate your salary.

§§§

Note: If you feel anxious in presenting and promoting yourself, asking and answering questions ... If you want to feel more confident in speaking with others and providing information about yourself, in general and in your job-getting campaign, be sure to check out my 10-module, 196-page guided, systematized home-study course, *Promote Myself? I'd Rather Eat Worms! 21 Simple Steps To Confidently Tooting Your Own Horn To Achieve Your Career and Life Goals.* It's available in Kindle on Amazon. http://tinyurl.com/bukudsr

5

YOU WANT TO TEST
MY "WHAT"?

Many companies include testing as part of their job-applicant screening process. All job applicants may be subjected to taking tests but applicants for executive, managerial, and professional jobs are often subjected to batteries of tests which can last from hours to days. Incredibly, sometimes spouses of applicants may be tested too. It has been estimated that more than a million of these tests are given by companies daily for one purpose or another.

The tests are wide-ranging. At any given time they may address psychological areas, such as aptitude, interest, personality, attitude, political or religious beliefs, intelligence, emotional intelligence, and skills. But they may also address such areas as honesty, drug usage, handwriting, and the presence of AIDS, pregnancy, or genetic conditions.

One such test is an examination of optimism. Currently over 50 insurance companies are using the Seligman Attributional Style Questionnaire (SASQ) to test for positive thinking. Based on work by Martin E.P. Seligman, Ph.D., a psychologist at the University of Pennsylvania and nationally-known expert on positive psychology, it has shown that optimism is highly correlated with success behavior.

The first company to use SASQ was MetLife. Initially Seligman convinced the insurance company to launch a pilot project designed to test 15,000 recruits with his 20-minute examination. Since the company is a strong believer that applicants with an upbeat attitude will be better salespeople, they've made the SASQ part of their hiring/screening process. The company estimated this practice would boost revenues in the tens of millions of dollars. Unlike so many other employment tests, this is one test that actually shows a valid correlation between an attitudinal quality and behavioral results.

Some companies utilize the controversial handwriting analysis among their battery of tests for upper-level managers and executives. From a several-paragraph sample, writing analysts look for 20-plus cursive characteristics alleged to determine dishonesty and deceptiveness. Called "crystal-ball gazing" by some critics, these hand writing tests have no empirical validity. In spite of that, companies are willing to pay between $100 and $500 per test rather than assume the individual is honest or monitor him or her to see if dishonesty occurs.

IS TESTING OPTIONAL

Many companies say their hiring decisions are based only *in part* upon these test results. And while a company may tell you that taking a test is *optional*, do NOT believe it. All too often the situation is that if you want to even be considered for the job, you HAVE to take the test(s).

I too have encountered this over and over. Many years ago I received a request from a company to set up a series of three interviews over a one-day period in three days' time for a marketing research position. The intensity of this interview process puzzled me because it was for a mid-level rather than an executive position. They said they'd fly me to New Jersey for interviews with the marketing department and other decision makers. However, these interviews would take place only after I had taken the B-SAT. The B-SAT was the Business Scholastic Aptitude Test, which ostensibly tested business aptitude and business knowledge.

I responded I'd be happy to meet with them (even on such short notice) and provide them with whatever verification of my credentials and demonstrations of my competencies they'd want. But ... at my professional level with all my experience I didn't feel comfortable taking an aptitude test. Something which I didn't tell them was that I felt it was a little insulting. Moreover, to take such a test which I knew nothing about I would have to prepare. I had no idea what the test would ask and how, in what format, and how I would be evaluated. There were no "Dummies" workbooks for B-SAT at the time.

I didn't want to take the test AND I didn't want to have to take it in order to be interviewed and evaluated for a job. That in combination with the normal amount of job-getting stress, not having been able to determine the actual decision maker, having to be flown to their out-of-state company, being interviewed by several decision makers (which can be very problematic if done in a group setting), and everything done all in one day wasn't going to work for me.

When I said I didn't wish to take the test, their response was ... (wait for it), "No test, no interviews!" For good or ill I chose not to test. So, there were no interviews. Taking their test was part of their employment "game" that I was not interested in playing. Even though they were a well-known international company, they seemed perhaps a little too inflexible for me.

There is a famous case wherein a company indicated all prospective employees had to take a test that asked very personal and inappropriate questions. The "validity" of their responses was to be "checked" by polygraph.

The questions included the following:

1. Are you homosexual?
2. What is your sexual preference?
3. Are you a Communist or revolutionary?
4. Do you get along with your spouse?
5. Do you drink alcohol?
6. Do you have money in the bank?
7. Are you in debt?
8. Do you attend church?
9. Have you ever stolen anything?

Prospective employees felt these questions were not

only degrading but also invading their privacy. As a result, the union workers struck the company. Critics of the testing indicated that what prospective employees did at work was certainly relevant to the company but what they did on their own time was NOT. The court ruled the test was an invasion of privacy and the plaintiffs won.

Unfortunately, over time things have changed. Many companies and organizations today increasingly intrude into their employees' lives, judging their acceptability as employees by their personal, private activities outside work. These include smoking cigarettes, drinking alcohol, smoking marijuana, gambling, partying, spending habits, sexual activities, relationships with neighbors, relationship with their spouse and/or family, and what employees may say or display on social media and sometimes in emails, even if unrelated to their work or the company.

In an economy where jobs are less plentiful, companies incredibly can and do almost anything they want. Interestingly, the use of tests in companies and organizations likewise has increased dramatically. These tests tend to be less bold than in the past but no less intrusive.

SHOULD YOU TAKE TESTS

There have been two schools of thought on that. One has said you can't beat the system. If taking the tests is what can potentially get you the job—the end justifies the means—why not do so. No harm done. But the other school of thought has said that if you've already demonstrated a high level of proficiency in your area, meet the job criteria, and have good references, it is demeaning for them to ask you to take these tests. However, sustaining such a principled position would mean having enough money in the bank money so you can eat and pay bills until you fund a position that doesn't require testing.

If you take the tests and don't get the job, you don't know if the test results were the deal breaker for you. You don't know what the test results "suggested" about you, how accurate or inaccurate, positive or negative they were. You don't know how valid and reliable those tests and their results were or if the test evaluator was properly trained. Your test results and their implications could then be out there for other potential employers to see and evaluate because companies may share candidate information.

Test proponents say that if you have an average IQ, job skills, and knowledge, you should be able to ace job-screening tests. However, critics see the majority of these tests as having little or no validity or reliability, depending upon their use. These tests can be used and relied upon for nearly anything the company wishes to employ them, whether ostensibly "designed" for that application or not. While the results of skills and IQ tests might not hurt your employment chances or affect your career, results of personality, aptitude, attitude, honesty, and drug testing, for example, might be another story.

PERSONALITY TESTS

A few years before the B-SAT incident, I had an interview for a similar job. Before I could see the interviewer, the receptionist told me to fill out the Adjective Check List, a personality test which lists 300 adjectives arranged in alphabetical order, from "absent-minded" to "zany." You're asked to mark all the adjectives you consider to be descriptive of yourself. When I returned a blank test form to the receptionist, she turned pale, obviously shocked, exclaiming, "You didn't fill it out. You *have* to fill it out. *Everyone* does."

Smiling, I said, "I'm sure many people do fill it out, but I don't feel comfortable doing so."

She hesitantly took the sheet in to the interviewer who then called me in. He shrugged his shoulders about it and put the sheet on his desk. The next thing I knew he was chuckling about some of the test's results the company had gotten over the years and what it said about those tested individuals. It was obvious this person had no qualms about breeching testing confidentiality.

That was bad enough but then he casually (wink, wink) shared with me some of the more "abnormal" details of the personality test results of the company's president. I was shocked to hear him do so ... and about the company's president! As was too often the case, this individual was unlikely to have been trained to interpret the results, understand and apply their meaning, then keep his mouth shut about them.

If he'd do it regarding the president of his company, why would I think my results would be confidential and not be chuckled over. There was an ethics problem there and no way to know how it reflected the company's attitude and how it operated. But it gave an uncomfortable inkling. Of course, I wasn't offered the job. But after the interviewer's actions, I definitely did not want it.

Personality tests are a strange collection of instruments. I know from having taken and researched them over the years. Some are objective while others are subjective. Some require you to mark answers on a sheet. Others ask you to respond to ambiguous pictures or ink blots, or ask you to draw figures. Some ask very personal questions about sexual, religious, and social beliefs, values, private behavior, honesty, fantasies, ethics, and feelings about your parents, to name only a few. Interestingly, if these questions were asked on a job application form or in an interview, they would be illegal but somehow when they're embedded in tests, they seem to get a pass.

The tests attempt to assess whether or not you are what the company considered their "expectations" of "normal"—whatever that is. And *if your results fit the corporate profile* (likewise, whatever that may be in any particular company), you have less to worry about.

But what if you have no particular problem but answer test questions in a way other than what they have determined fits within the "normal range"? It's important to remember that the majority of these tests were constructed between the 1930s and 1960s. Cultural values, beliefs, and the range of acceptability in many areas have changed since then.

For example, today it is generally considered "normal" for women to want to take on management and leadership roles. In gender-biased tests if females answer in a stereotypically socially acceptable "feminine" way, they'll likely be perceived as acting "appropriately" for females but, likewise, as weak and ineffectual when compared with the male as standard. If they respond instead in a less stereotypical fashion, which shows them as assertive, decision making, and leader-like, they likely will be seen as more like males, strong and effective, but acting "inappropriately" for being females, as noted earlier. Sad to say, some of that gender stereotyping may still exist in versions of these tests.

From the large number of diverse tests that are given, it's apparent that decision makers are no longer taking upon themselves the full responsibility for assessing candidates. It's no longer a matter of a candidate's performance, expertise, experience, skills, education, and previous results achieved. Instead they're relying more and more upon what the tests say. Why? It's easier, quicker, and the decision maker doesn't bear the onus of any "miscalculations" about a potential employee. If something goes awry with a new employee, the decision maker has an old reliable to blame: "The test results made me do it."

The reason companies are relying upon tests is that tests "look" scientific. They look "objective." They "claim" to predict a vast array of information about the individual. They "claim" to predict how well the individual will do with the company. They also assert that the company couldn't collect this "information" any other way. The problem, however, is that this claim is very difficult to prove so they just go on testing.

PROBLEMS WITH EMPLOYMENT TESTS

Tests used as employment tests are often misused, misapplied. Too often those who interpret these tests to label a job applicant as "fit" or "unfit" for the job and company are untrained or poorly trained. Too often the so-called "confidentiality" of individuals' test results is lacking or poorly controlled.

Are tests really *that* bad? Yes, some actually are. How bad they are depends upon what tests the company gives you in their screening. Some tests are more culturally-biased than others. Some are more gender-biased. This can significantly affect different ethnic, racial, and gender groups. Fortunately, not all companies use testing. However, the majority do use it, especially large corporations. So, you're likely to confront the "no test, no job" mentality until testing falls from grace or simply goes out of vogue. This, however, is unlikely to happen because of testing's cachet, simplicity, and ease of use.

For some people the *to-test-or-not-to-test decision* will be a tough one to make. But most people who want and need a job will understandable do whatever is necessary to comply with the company's demands to get it. If you choose to take these tests, your best protection is to prepare yourself for them.

Aside from those that specifically assess your math and verbal skills, your knowledge of a particular subject area, the remainder will look at your personal activities, preferences, values, beliefs, and how well what you do and think *conforms* to what's considered "socially desirable" by that company.

PLAYING THE TESTING GAME

If you're going to take tests in hopes of getting a job, you're going to have to learn how to play the game. From your own job-related market research (industry, company, job, and decision maker) you should have some inkling, though it's often hard to find out, of the psychology and character of the organization asking you to test.

Unless the potential employer is a "maverick" like Google or Ben & Jerry's Ice Cream Company, it is likely to look for a fit to the profile known as "conservative big business." This profile presents the ideal employee as one who is self-confident, hard-driving, unemotional, dominant, and responsible. It also looks for one who is cooperative, loyal to the end, a team player, and may be "anti-cultural."

While corporations may publicly assert they value "flexibility," this may not necessarily reflect their real corporate environment. Corporate America is quite conservative.   As a result, some companies may be less concerned about social responsibility, employee rights and benefits, ethics, and a creative environment. Instead, they may be concerned with profit to the extent of valuing the ends over of the means used to achieve them. These are things you should know and for which you should look for clues in your information research on the company.

If you have decided it is to your benefit to test because the company and job are what you want, you need to determine how to structure your image through their testing so it reflects the company's philosophy, psychology, and approach.

As you can guess, test items tend to reflect the company's orientation. For example, if on a test you are given the choice of visiting an art museum or a medical laboratory, for most companies you would be expected to pick the laboratory. The art museum is too qualitative and subjective whereas the laboratory is quantitative and objective. This is, of course, unless the organization specifically represents the arts, their associations, and alliances in some way.

If you're asked how often you call your mother, you should say "infrequently" because a close relationship with one's mother tends to be seen as being "less serious" for a woman and "Oedipal" for a man. Moreover, calling frequently or daily might be construed as you having your thoughts, concerns, and interests slanted toward home rather than toward the job.

If asked about religion, you should say you believe in a Supreme Being and attend church once a week. This is whether you do or not. Believing in a Supreme Being is supposed to be a given. To attend church less than once a week tends to make you a "free thinker" in some companies. To attend church more than once a week tends to make you a "zealot" in some companies *unless* the company leans toward evangelic or orthodox religion. This is unless, of course, the job is associated in some way with that religion. Then your answer would be what your religion would consider appropriate.

If presented with the choice of playing basketball or reading the Bible, you should choose basketball. Basketball is an outgoing, athletic, competitive, and more masculine-stereotype activity whereas reading the Bible is more introspective and uncompetitive. This is, again, unless the company or organization emphasizes that it has a strict religious orientation. As you can see, if you answer as you would as a unique individual with many interests—not necessarily as some idealized construct, you may not be valued for the competent, experienced individual you are.

For some people the idea of having to "lie" about your real thoughts, beliefs, attitudes, interests, personality, characteristics, and behaviors in order to "give them what they want" is annoying, chafing, and immoral. It can certainly make you wonder how much the company will value the *real* you and the *real* way you think and do things. But, then again, it is a game. If you feel you will fit comfortably with the job and company, and there are no good alternatives, you should consider playing the game and getting the benefits you want for your efforts.

FREQUENT TEST FORMATS

What kinds of test formats can you expect to encounter? Some present you with a forced-choice where you can pick only an absolute:

1. Yes or no
2. True or false
3. All or nothing.

When you answer these questions, you need to consider how society would expect you to respond, given the culture's norms, mores, and beliefs. This means you need to read each question carefully for key words, such as "ever," "never," "often," "rarely," "occasionally," "frequently," "constantly," "always."

For example, "Do you *ever* think about hurting people?" Since most people have probably thought of "harming" someone (at least in a minor way) at one time or another, you could answer, "Yes." If, however, you answered, "No," because it isn't something you have done with any intensity or frequency or you believe it's immoral to do so, you might be taken for a liar or someone unaware of your own impulses. If however, it said, "Do you *often* think about hurting people?" you'd want to respond, "No."

In general, you want to go for the middle ground. If you choose the "socially desirable" answer which is oriented to the company profile, you should choose "frequently." For "socially <u>un</u>desirable" items, you would choose "rarely" *unless* it's something the average person is likely never to have done. As a general rule, *avoid* extremes, as in "always" and "never." For most people these words don't describe their behavior, whether good or bad. Questions are often going to be repeated throughout the test in different forms as a control for people trying to "beat the test." Therefore, you need to be aware of this and make a point to answer consistently, keeping social stereotypes in mind.

One problem for any test taker is that everything is a matter of interpretation. That is, some tests may present you with premises that aren't valid for you but will then ask you questions about them. One test I took as part of a research project in which I was participating said, "When I cheat at cards, I feel ...." I was supposed to check off the appropriate adjective.

As you might guess from my previous responses, I found this really irksome. As a result, I wrote over the question, "The premise is invalid. I've never cheated at cards"—which I never had. Of course, what they wanted you to do was ask yourself, "IF I had cheated at cards, how would I feel?" then give the socially desirable answer, "I'd feel guilty."

Obviously, it's not always easy to determine what

testers are looking for or what they will judge as a socially desirable "correct" response. This means you have two choices. You can respond to "if" and "when" situations as if the question were a hypothetical, as what they apparently wanted me to do. Or, you can respond that since that type of question doesn't apply to you, you're not responding—but this is a *bad* idea. Talking back to the question likely makes you seem as too independent, not a company person, perhaps hostile, and maybe even a rabble-rouser or troublemaker. Furthermore, you'd be thinking for and about yourself and not for or about the company.

HONESTY TESTS

Since many companies are increasingly concerned about business ethics of their employees, such as theft and industrial espionage, they are likely to be trying to determine your honesty. Or they may be trying to ascertain if you're an ethical person who would feel guilty about breaking even a seemingly minor moral law.

Until December 27, 1988, when Congress banned employers' use of polygraph tests, voice-stress analyzers, and other electronic methods (The Employee Polygraph Protection Act), so-called "lie detectors" were used routinely to screen prospective and current workers. The U.S. Department of Labor details the law as follows:

"The Employee Polygraph Protection Act prohibits most private employers from using lie detector tests, either for pre-employment screening or during the course of employment. Employers generally may not require or request any employee or job applicant to take a lie detector test, or discharge, discipline, or discriminate against an employee or job applicant for refusing to take a test or for exercising other rights under the Act.

"Employers may not use or inquire about the results of a lie detector test or discharge or discriminate against an employee or job applicant on the basis of the results of a test, or for filing a complaint, or for participating in a proceeding under the Act. Subject to restrictions, the Act permits polygraph (a type of lie detector) tests to be administered to certain job applicants of security service firms (armored car, alarm, and guard) and of pharmaceutical manufacturers, distributors and dispensers."

[Even though they are not listed, government agencies may also require a polygraph test for employment. There are, of course, other provisos for the use of a polygraph.]

"Subject to restrictions, the Act also permits polygraph testing of certain employees of private firms who are reasonably suspected of involvement in a workplace incident (theft, embezzlement, etc.) that resulted in specific economic loss or injury to the employer. Where polygraph examinations are allowed, they are subject to strict standards for the conduct of the test, including the pretest, testing and post-testing phases. An examiner must be licensed and bonded or have professional liability coverage. The Act strictly limits the disclosure of information obtained during a polygraph test."

Even though most employers have been banned from using a polygraph in hiring, you have to be on the alert because occasionally a company, other than those exempted by the law, will try to circumvent the law by requiring its job applicants take a polygraph test.

The rationale for employers' use of polygraphs was "protection of profit margins." According to the Commerce Department, each year U.S. business loses upwards of $50 billion to employee theft (other estimates range as high as $200 billion). It is a tremendous and costly problem, especially for stores and warehouses.

Even though crime and lawyer dramas frequently talk about having a suspect take a polygraph, polygraph usage was discontinued as a screening instrument by law enforcement because of the lack of proof of the scientific validity of these devices—that these devices can actually detect what they claim to detect. That is why courts will not accept results of a polygraph tests. These tests offer no indication of truth or lying, guilt or innocence. Police tend to believe in and rely upon them all the same.

PROBLEMS WITH POLYGRAPH TESTS

First, massive amounts of research have shown that the polygraph does *not* detect lies or dishonesty. Instead, it merely records signs of anxiety or physiological symptoms of stress, such as increased pulse, breathing rate, and perspiration.

As you know, anxiety and stress aren't limited to lying behavior. In fact, some people feel no anxiety or stress when lying. However:

. Many people have anxiety about taking any kind of test.
. This is especially true of a machine that they may believe can potentially reveal unrelated secrets.

. Being strapped into a chair with a coil around your chest and a clip on your finger, with wires all around, being electronically connected to the machine is intimidating.

. Individuals may tend to think of past, albeit minor, indiscretions and embarrassments and worry that they might come out.

. They may feel guilty about something they have done which is totally unrelated to the situation at hand.

. Some may be worried that the test can actually see into their heads to read their thoughts and feelings.

Consider how you'd respond if asked, "Have you ever stolen *any*thing from your employer?" Your first thought would be, "No!" But wait a minute. Your mind might suddenly recall when you occasionally made some personal copies on the company copier. The company had a policy about personal copies and you didn't ask permission or pay the company back. It was so trivial. Still it could be called "stealing." But as insignificant as it seems to be, you may suddenly *think* about it. Doing so raises your blood pressure and stress level, perhaps suggesting you're lying about whatever was just asked.

Second, these tests have been found to harm individuals by falsely implicating them. One such incident concerned J.J.O., a ten-year veteran of a large restaurant chain. He was an area supervisor in charge of 28 restaurants and 500 employees. He was in line for the position of vice-president. However, when he wouldn't promote the son of a company director (who was also the godson of the company president), he was anonymously accused of taking drugs at an off-hours party. The company threatened, "Take a polygraph or be fired." Coerced, he anxiously took it and the test found him "lying" and "guilty." He was fired. Feeling indignant at being falsely accused, he sued. A federal jury found the company's investigation "highly offensive" and awarded J.J.O. close to a million dollars.

Does this mean that companies can no longer test for honesty? No. They still can and do. However, when the polygraph examinations disappeared, a multitude of paper-and-pencil exams appeared to fill the void. In fact, millions of these tests were given to job applicants starting in 1988, on the heels of the termination of polygraph examinations.

AFTER POLYGRAPHS, WHAT

Again, companies like and rely on the paper-and-pencil honesty tests. They are increasingly popular because of their:

. Perceived validity
. Aura of reliability
. Legal defensibility
. Cost-effectiveness.

What do these tests ask you? For example:

. "Do you always tell the truth?"
. "If you are like most others, you have stolen something in the past. What was your reason?"
. "Would you tell your boss if you knew of another employee stealing from the company?"

These are difficult questions, especially asking if you'd tell your boss about someone else stealing from the company. This is a situation which is full of conflict for lots of reasons. Even though reporting a crime is considered responsible, ethical behavior, which they would expect you to do, there could be personal repercussions to consider if you were placed in such a position. For example:

. How would your colleagues likely regard you?
. Would they be concerned about sharing personal information or work concerns with you?
. How might the company and colleagues' reactions affect your overall job performance?
. What the company might expect of you in the future.

There is one way to absolutely "flunk" honesty tests. If your responses suggest you:

. Rationalize theft with "everybody does it" generalizations
. Believe that most employees are dishonest and steal.

But, of course, believing either or both of those statements does *not* mean you are more likely to be dishonest and steal. As you can see, there are problems with honesty tests.

Critics have found that honesty tests yield a high number of "false-negative" scores—scores which label individuals as "high risk" (potentially dishonest) when, in fact, they are not. One assessment of the frequency of "false-negative" scores was above 67%.

The U.S. Office of Technology Assessment in 1990 found these tests to have considerable negative effects on those tested. One such negative effect is racial and sexual discrimination. As a result, numbers of states have banned the use of such tests, with perhaps only 15% of companies now using them. But these statistics tend to change over time so it is difficult to know what the current situation is unless you research it for specific companies. And even then, it will be hard to ascertain which companies do and get an accurate percentage. This means you may encounter one or more of these tests or not.

DRUG TESTS

Because drug abuse costs American industry in excess of $100 billion annually in absenteeism, turnover, reduced productivity, and increased accidents, employers increasingly are using drug testing irrespective of the type or size of business. Consequently, no employer wants to hire someone who is *likely* to use drugs or alcohol at work ... or even off-work on their personal time. The following will cover the various aspects of drugs tests as they apply to pre-employment testing.

The U.S. Supreme Court has held that it is not harmful to job applicant' privacy to have their blood and urine collected. In general, it may be considered an invasion of privacy to have others watching during collection, unless the company can demonstrate concern about tampering. Where such a concern exists, they may have another person of the same sex observe.

Specific federal agencies or departments may have drug-testing policies in place, as will any employer who receives federal grants or contracts. Each state has its own laws concerning drug testing. In many, the employer has the right to test for drugs and alcohol as long as the job applicants understand that testing is part of the interview, or pre-employment, process.

The Americans with Disabilities Act (ADA) prohibits pre-employment medical examinations before a *conditional offer* of employment has been extended. Therefore, no testing is allowed *before* the offer to those with disabilities. Furthermore, the employer must treat all job applicants for the same job equally. They cannot select who should or should not be tested.

Drug testing has some limitations by state statute. Specifically, there may be limits on the types of testing that can be performed. Currently tests cover blood, urine, breath, and hair. These tests cannot legally be done covertly. That is, the employer cannot simply use saliva left on a soda can or hair left on a chair during the interview to test. The applicant has to *know* what the employer is doing and *choose* to go along with it or not.

Drug test results can take anywhere from a few hours to several weeks to a month and may cover many drugs. Basic drug test panels target:

. Marijuana
. Hashish
. Cocaine
. Crack
. Heroin
. Opium
. Codeine
. Morphine

. Amphetamines
. Methamphetamines
. Speed
. PCP.
   There is also a larger panel that includes:
. Phenobarbital
. Secobarbitol
. Pentobarbital
. Butalbital
. Amobarbital
. Qualuude
. Tranquilizers (Valium, Librium, Halcion, Ativan, Serax, Xanax, Klonopin)
. Rohypnol
. Methadone
. Darvon compounds
. Alcohol
. LSD
. Psilocybin
. Mescaline
. MDMA ("Ecstasy")
. MDA ("Sally"- amphetamine class)
. MDE ("Eve" – phenylamine and amphetamine classes)
. Inhalants (toluene, xylene, benzene).

Furthermore, testing must have written policies which are made known to job applicants as well as to employees about what kind of drug testing is done, when it will take place, and how it will be performed. Employers are *expected* to exercise discretion with respect to drug test results and provide them on a "need-to-know" basis *only*.

It's important to note that the error rate for drug testing analysis can be as high as 14% depending upon the drug for which the analysis is being done.   Some over-the-counter drugs can create false-positive results:

. Ibuprophen (Advil, Motrin)
. Sudafed,
. Vicks 44
. Vicks Nasal Spray
. Neosynephren
. Dextromethorphan
. Nuprin
. Midol
. Ephedra.

If you've taken any of these medications and are scheduled to be tested, you need to make sure you tell the employer so that they can do a re-test if you get a "positive" result on your first test.

This is an area wherein there used to be some question about the constitutionality of what was seen from the individual's perspective as *invasion of privacy, illegal search and seizure,* and *denial of the principle of probable cause.* But over the years the pendulum has swung away from individual rights to company rights.

What this means is that even if you take all their drug tests, there is still no guarantee that you'll get the job. And there's no guarantee that the next company at which you apply for a job will not have heard about your previous drug test results, whether they're accurate or inaccurate.

MEDICAL AND GENETICS SCREENINGS

Genetic screening has become part of the stable of tests employers can use to screen candidates. Prior to 2008 there existed only a patchwork of state laws which regulated the discriminatory use of genetic information. In May of 2008 the Genetic Information Nondiscrimination Act (GINA) was passed. It made it illegal for employers or health insurers (but *not* life insurers) to discriminate against individuals based on their genetic information. Genetic information cannot be part of the underwriting of health insurance plans. And, specifically, now employers cannot make hiring, firing, or promotion decisions using your genetic information.

In the past many who could have benefited from it (for detecting disease, predicting possible future disease, guiding treatment options, and informing reproductive decisions) were afraid to have genetic testing done because the information could be used against them ... and often was. There are currently about 1,200 diseases for which there are genetic tests.

Some of the genetic tests deal with a *predisposition* to a disease. That is, there may be a genetic configuration that suggests that you have the *potential* later in life for having a particular disease, *but* that there's no way to know if you will *actually* contract it or if you're an unaffected carrier of DNA that could be passed on to your children or not. There is still some concern about the employer or others doing genetic testing, analysis, and dissemination of the resulting confidential information without the individual's permission. Protections for this may be limited and vary by state. You would need to check out your state.

With respect to AIDS, the Americans with Disabilities Act protects individuals with AIDS, guaranteeing job rights to people with "handicaps." However, there have been cases where people with AIDS have had their privacy invaded by their company and were fired because of their test results. There have been instances of pregnancy testing the urine of women job applicants, without their permission, resulting in a job rejection of a woman with apparent positive test results.

There is also the idea that some individuals may be genetically more sensitive to toxic or pathogenic effects of environmental agents. Employers, therefore, have in the past suggested that occupational genetic screening would "benefit workers" by *allowing* the company to determine work places that are safest for them. Employers have also said that knowing this information would ensure that those susceptible to certain occupational diseases would not be put in the "wrong" work environments. What this meant is that employers could, under the cloak of paternalism, refuse employment to those they considered most likely to contract a particular occupational disease irrespective of the potential employee's choice and decision.

In one case in order for women to retain a high-paying factory job which exposed them to lead, they had to agree to be sterilized. However, there was no such requirement for men who would equally be exposed to lead, its toxicity, and negative reproductive effects. So the men were eligible for the higher-paying jobs but the women weren't unless they gave up their reproductive rights.

By exempting particularly susceptible workers, many industries argued that there was no need for stricter standards of exposure to toxic agents. Therefore, rather than removing these occupational health hazards from the workplace, businesses wanted to merely fire those would were likely to be affected, or not hire those most likely to be affected. Everyone else (men, not women) could choose to take their chances and be well-compensated for it. This was taking the decision of where to work out of the employees' hands in order to maximize profits. Now, in general, industries are *expected* to provide safer workplaces for *all,* though they do not necessarily do it.

Furthermore, all potential hires have to be informed before employment of any potential dangers in the specific job or workplace in general so the employees themselves can decide to take the risk or not. However, there still may be vestiges of this former problem as law and regulations change. This is something of which you need to be aware.

Note: Hiring or not hiring because of workplace dangers is not specifically an Occupational Health and Safety Act (OSHA) issue. Instead it likely falls under the Federal Equal Employment Opportunity (EEOC) and Americans with Disabilities Act (ADA) under the area of "reasonable accommodation."

CREDIT BUREAUS AND SEARCH AGENCIES

Some employers will not hire a candidate until they have also reviewed that individual's credit history—something which used to be private and unrelated to your job abilities. Companies such as Trans Union (formerly TRW), the largest supplier of consumer credit information, sell information on the potential employee's bank account, outstanding bills, credit score, tax liens and bankruptcies all of which may be—and often are—replete with errors. Trans Union has numerous data banks which contain any kind of profile a company might want on a potential employee: the individual's tastes, lifestyle, expenditures, voting record, and medical history.

Equifax, another well-known information provider, has said in the past that they've found that at least 11% of applicants misstated their reason for having left their prior position, 3% gave false academic credentials, and another 3% claimed they had worked for companies for which they hadn't. As companies have downsized and the economy has had its difficulties off and on, the incidence of providing inaccurate information has increased significantly—making both the inaccurate information and the potential employer seeking your credit and other history a common occurrence.

At one time criminal histories, not only convictions but also simple arrests (mistaken or not) could be gotten from the Federal Bureau of Investigation's Identification Division. This database covers many millions of people. Today, private search companies can provide nearly *any* piece of information an employer might want regarding a potential employee. Because companies can be held liable for the crimes of their employees, companies feel justified in knowing anything and everything about the public and private lives of their employees. In many instances, the employee has very little privacy and even less control of it.

You may find it to your advantage to check with the three primary credit bureaus to check your current credit information:

. Trans Union (http://www.transunion.com/)
. Equifax (http://www.equifax.com/)
. Experian (http://www.experian.com/).

You'll want to check your credit and other history files, particularly if you have ever experienced any previous credit problems or unexplained changes. Often these files contain errors which are correctable and need to be corrected as soon as possible. Most of these services allow you to pay to access your files. It is advisable that you know at least as much as a potential employer who can and likely will gain access to this data. This would allow you to prepare yourself with counter-measures for any unpleasant surprises.

MAKING YOUR TESTING DECISION

We've come a long way from the time when getting a job depended mainly upon your work record, references, and the interview. As you can see, all the different kinds of testing and investigation available that are used today make it more complex for you to get the job you want.

Whereas at one time you had some flexibility about what tests you were willing to take, today you have very little or none if you want to be considered for a job. That decision has, in effect, been taken out of your hands.

If you can determine in advance what is required for pre-employment screening, it may provide you with some basis for assessing the company's philosophy, psychological slant, rigidity or flexibility, policies, and practices. It can allow you to decide for yourself how much of your privacy you're willing to give up in order to be *considered* for a particular position, either before or after the interview.

Just keep in mind that acing your employment tests does not guarantee you anything—the same way having the interview does not guarantee you anything. So, if you've done your research, feel you are *simpatico* with the company, and are willing to take this risk (no matter how much or how little), taking employment tests will at least give you a chance at being hired.

Even though testing is an important component of the employer's decision about you, what will likely guide their thinking and decision making about your candidacy is:

. How you have marketed yourself.
. How you have presented and promoted yourself
. How your presentation and image matched what they're looking for will likely supersede many other considerations.

Of course, this is as long as there's no large problem lurking in any of your test results, your credit report, or references.

WHAT IF YOU GET A REJECTION LETTER

If you receive a rejection letter, all is not necessarily lost. Since these letters ordinarily do not spell out why you did not get the job, it might be a good idea to follow up on this. It's important to know why you weren't chosen: Was it your credentials or your presentation? Was there not really an opening? Or was there a glitch you may still be able to correct?

Contacting the decision maker, you could say that even though you "weren't offered the job," you still feel you're the right person for it and company. Then ask if he or she will share with you why you weren't the one. Unless the decision maker tells you something that can't be corrected, you can tell him or her that you want to demonstrate how you can contribute. Specifically, you want to provide them with a *free* "project consultation" on a non-proprietary problem on which they're working.

That is, the decision maker would provide you with an outline of the problem, what's been done to date, the resources that are available for it, any other relevant information, and a time frame for your solution. This freebie would be hard for the company to refuse.

Providing the company with a new set of eyes on a problem is a practical, effective, and efficient way to show your seriousness about wanting to work for that company. It would let the decision maker see first-hand what you can do. If they still haven't filled the position for which you applied, you would be more likely to be reconsidered if you performed well. If they have already filled the first position, you likely would be in a better place for consideration for the next similar opening that occurs there.

Some people have suggested that you offer the company a three-month internship *at that job level* for *free.* It would have to be at that position level because you want to be able to demonstrate your skills and experience, and learning. However, depending upon the field and company, the internship may work better for students who will be graduated soon than for adults.

Signe A. Dayhoff, PhD

Research has shown that for students the internship should *not* be free but paid, making the students after graduation more likely get a job and get a higher salary. Internships are an excellent way for newbies in the field to learn more about working in their field and in specific companies.

At the very least, if your "project consultation" or internship doesn't result in a job offer, you will have gotten to know the company and its people. You will have been able to network with people of influence. You will have the experience to put on your résumé. When asked about it at your next interview, you can say you were interested in that company and wanted to learn more up-close and personal. It shows initiative.

Of course, if you can be paid in some way, that would be even more beneficial in all respects, especially since the payment aspect attaches a greater value to your time and effort. However, your willingness to demonstrate your potential contribution will help you be seen as a go-getter who will climb over, dig under, or go around any obstacle in your path to achieve your goal.

TEMPORARY JOB ALTERNATIVES

While you're between interviews, if you haven't found a free or paid consulting job or internship with the company you can use (to continue to learn, grow, and develop), there are other options available to you. You can:

1. Take a course(s) or seminar(s) at your local college or university on an area (or areas) that will further enhance your skill set and expertise.

2. Work on a project with someone well-known in your field.

3. Offer paid or free adult education course on one of your areas of expertise. It can be at a local college, at a vocational school, or at a community center.

4. Counsel high school students on your area of experience.

5. Counsel students, adults, or veterans on job getting, especially in your area of expertise.

6. Provide paid workshops for lower-level workers in your field for their companies.

7. Coach or mentor managers in your field on some aspect of what you do that would be a valuable addition to their on-going education.

8. Write articles on trends in your field.

All of these, and many more, can help you:

1. Keep from having a large unemployment gap

2. Keep your information and skills up-to-date

3. Contribute to your community

4. Be seen as an educator, coach, advisor, counselor, or mentor

5. Be viewed as socially responsible

6. Add to your image and your résumé.

6

YOU'VE GOTTEN THE JOB OFFER: NOW WHAT?

Now that you've garnered at least one job offer, you have decisions to make. "Oh, no!" you say, "I thought getting the offer was it—the only decision I'd have to make is to say, 'Yes.'"

In reality, at this point you have to decide exactly what will be the best deal for you. This means you need to consider all the factors—and there are many—involved in accepting an offer because you want to be sure you will get what you want the way you want it. And it is important to remember that this is increasingly the case as you move up the corporate ladder. The higher the level the more there is to consider.

In most cases, except perhaps at entry-level, the corporate expectation is that you will not immediately accept. You will likely want 24 hours in which to mull over the offer and your situation. At higher levels you likely may take up to 48 hours in which to decide. This, of course, will vary from company to company. However, it is usually considered common courtesy to extend you at least the 24 hours in which to make your decision.

WHAT YOU NEED TO ASSESS

1. You need to concretely assess how the offer fits in with your priorities:
   a. Career goals
   b. Job wants
   c. Professional values
   d. Financial needs.
2. You need to compare this offer to any other offers you may be considering.
3. You need to assess how well you relate to the decision maker with whom you'll be working and to whom you'll report.
4. You need to ask yourself specifically:
   a. Do you feel comfortable with this decision maker as a boss?
   b. Can you communicate openly and easily?
   c. Do you feel compatible with their work style and personality?
   d. Is this person someone you feel you can trust?
   e. Are you comfortable with this company's philosophy, overall attitudes, ethics, and behaviors toward employees as well as customers/clients?

Once you have thought those factors over, you can do one of four (4) things. Specifically you can:

1. Accept the salary-only offer as is (generally *not* a good

idea—we'll go into this in a moment)

2. Negotiate to get as much of what you want in salary (before you know about the compensation package—generally *not* a good idea)

3. Turn the salary offer down.

4. Wait ... to learn *all* that your offer's compensation includes.

DON'T ACCEPT THE OFFER JUST YET

You want the offer to reflect your experience and expertise and what is the going rate for that type of position in the market place. Chances are good that the salary being offered may not meet your expectations based upon your research. Don't let this concern you. The company may try to get you for less.

For this reason, it is useful to have a carefully calculated counter-offer in mind. In fact, employers may anticipate a counter-offer so they will leave room for negotiation with respect to salary. You can let them know that "you understand that they are in a better position to evaluate how much you are worth to the company than you are. Furthermore, given that, you will consider any 'reasonable' offer."

This means that if the company offers you X and you feel based on your experience you should get Y, you should express that using several reference points. For example, you might say, "With the 20 years of experience I bring to your company as well what others in similar positions in similar companies are making, I believe your offer is on the conservative side." (Notice how diplomatically this is expressed.)

Remember. You are negotiating for what you "want"

based upon (1) what you bring to the position and (2) what is typical across the industry, and *not* on what you "need." So you always want to maintain the quietly confident attitude that you are the one *they* need it and the company is lucky to get you.

Note: If you suddenly discover that what you were willing to accept salary-wise is too little for the actual position, all is not necessarily lost. Suck up your mistake and indicate that "now that you know more specific details about the job itself, the level of the position, and the breadth of its responsibilities, you feel the earlier figure is no longer relevant. Based on your research on salaries for similar positions with all that is required and expected, you want the salary figure to be adjusted accordingly."

If you think everything is fine with the salary offer as it is made to you (with or without adjustment), you still should *not* accept it on the spot. Companies tend to expect you to follow professional protocol: discuss salary *and* compensation and then wait to decide on the final offer.

If you don't, the decision maker may perceive you as too eager. If you seem too "hungry," this can be a turn off for the employer. Or, they could see you as just truly enthusiastic and ready to give your all to the company.

Taking their offer is supposed to be a serious decision and serious decisions take a little time. This is even after you and the employer have discussed and agreed upon your salary and other compensations that go with the job. (This discussion and agreement are absolutely imperative *before* you sign a contract.)

Throughout the entire job-getting process, you need to

maintain your image as thoughtful, cool, and professional. As the end nears, you do not want to appear impulsive, even if you had decided ages ago this is the job you wanted and you can't wait to get this process over with. You also do *not* want to appear as if you have no other offers. Remember: It's not that you "need" the job. Desperation is not an attractive quality in anyone and especially not to potential employers.

WHAT ABOUT COMPENSATION PACKAGES

Compensation? You might have thought that was just what you were going to be paid as salary. But there's more—much more—to it. Compensation comes in packages, little ones and big ones, depending upon your job level and the company. This means you need to know about what is being offered at that company for that job.

Once you're offered the position, you need to ask for a *complete description* of what the compensation package that goes along with the job contains. Irrespective of level and type of full-time job, there will be a compensation package. You need to know what is possible for that company, job level, and position. And even if you have discovered the information on your own or the interviewer or decision maker has provided it, you and the employer need to discuss it so that you and the employer are on the same page during your compensation negotiation.

Never forget that the compensation of one $30,000-per year job may outweigh the compensation of another $30,000-per year job. This is why you need to consider this carefully and need to actively negotiate.

There are four (4) categories of compensation: Money,

benefits, perquisites, and status.

1. _Money_ consists of salary, bonuses, negotiated raises, commissions, stock options, profit sharing, and deferred profit sharing.
2. _Benefits_ consist of health insurance, dental plan, pension, and vacation time. Depending upon your level, they also may offer sick, maternity, and family time days. Re-location expenses may be included.
3. _Perquisites_ consist of expense account, credit cards, company car, club membership, parking, and company products and/or services.
4. _Status_ consists of office size and location and the use of a secretary and/or assistant.

From your research you need to have a ball park idea of what each compensation item is worth. Aside from salary, the most negotiable items are:

. Bonus
. Commissions
. Vacations
. Expense account
. Automobile
. Parking
. Size and location of the office
. Use of a secretary.

BE PREPARED TO NEGOTIATE

Before you can negotiate a salary you have to have a really solid idea what _you_ are worth. This determination depends upon a lot of factors, starting with the industry, the company and its size, the company's geographical location, the job level, and the economy. It also depends upon what history, education, experience, skills, interpersonal communications abilities, and personality you bring to the table. Research has shown that the better your interpersonal communication skills and your positive personality, the better your salary.

To have a better idea what you are "worth," you need to:

1. Research what salaries are assigned to similar jobs through trade journals, business periodicals, and newspaper classified ads
2. Check for salary surveys online (Salary.com; PayScale.com)
3. Check on this company's financial situation to see if they are stable, doing well, about to expand, merging, and have some salary flexibility
4. Network to see what others in the same field get as well as what they perceive as the going rate for that job and for someone with your background
5. Do an objective personal assessment of what you offer.

You also have to have a good sense of what the individual items in the compensation are worth. You can't negotiate with them if their assigned value is unknown. You can't intelligently decide what to do after negotiation without that information.

Negotiating is a respectful win-win process whereby each participant comes away a winner with something they want. By negotiating, you demonstrate that you know and have important business, interpersonal, and communication skills that you will be using on the job.

A simple, non-business example of negotiation: Ajay and Samantha finish dinner and Ajay says, "I want the baklava we picked up yesterday." Samantha agrees. As she gets the large piece and two plates, she says, "Let's cut it down the center." Ajay looks disappointed, "You want half, not just a sliver?" Samantha replies, "You cut the baklava into two pieces any way you like but then I get to choose which piece I want." While Ajay really wants most of it, if he got half, at least it would be his decision to divide the pastry evenly. Samantha's solution has an element of fairness so he agrees.

Negotiating is something you do every day. It's what occurs in any relationships. You do it to make the best deal you can in buying a car, deciding where to go for dinner, attempting to convince a child to eat its greens, or getting the job compensation you want. This calm, respectful back-and-forth communication is designed to achieve agreement when you share interests with others but not necessarily their perceptions, goals, and needs. Since you want to participate in decisions which affect your life, you try your best to influence those decisions so they turn out in your favor to the greatest degree possible.

Negotiating is difficult when you have not been trained how to do it. As a result, often your attempts likely have been ineffective and may have left you feeling frustrated, dissatisfied, and unhappy with yourself, others, and the end result. This tends to happen when you are:

1. Eager to avoid personal conflict and make concessions

to reach an agreement which leaves you feeling angry and exploited later.
2. Willing to win at any cost and damage the relationship in the process.

For negotiation to work it is better to seek a middle ground. That is, after you decide on the merits of the issues, you look for *mutual* gain. Good negotiation should produce a win-win agreement that is efficient and does not harm the relationship. Several tips to help you negotiate:

. Know precisely what you want, prepare accordingly by listing points you want to make.
. Know what the other wants, their strengths, weaknesses, and interests so you can anticipate reactions and emphasize benefits to them.
. Negotiate face to face.
. Do not bargain over position because it results in a battle of wills reducing your flexibility.
. Know the *what, how, why,* and *why not* of the other's interests because interests define the problem.
. Separate the person from the problem.
. Show sensitivity, empathy, and understanding to make the process smoother.
. Create flexible options for resolution that create mutual gain.
. Acknowledge and bring to light what individual interests are seen as part of the problem.
. Dovetail differing interests where possible.
. Use only objective, concrete, and specific criteria that can be agreed upon.

. Get areas of minor agreement dispensed with as early as possible to set a positive tone for the rest of the negotiation.

. Expect silence and be comfortable with it.

. Expect the other may have emotional outbursts and do not respond.

. Deep-six blaming the other for the problem.

. Make proposals that are consistent with the other's values and interests.

. When solution is agreed upon, clearly outline the agreement: Who does what, when, and the expected result.

. Make sure both parties have a common understanding of your agreement.

. End on a positive note, emphasizing the progress made and how each person worked hard to achieve that end.

John F. Kennedy said, "Let us begin anew, remembering on both sides that civility is not a sign of weakness, that sincerity is always subject to proof. Let us never negotiate out of fear. But let us never fear to negotiate."

Companies have numerous expectations of those to whom they offer a job. One of those expectations is that you will negotiate on your salary and compensation package. If for some reason you do not, they may wonder why you don't. After all, smart, savvy people know that in most cases this is what you should do in this business situation.

During the salary discussion, you may be asked what you made on your previous job. Do *not* reveal your previous salary because this is *not* relevant to your new position. Career counselors may vary on this but keep in mind that this *new* position is

1. At a different company
2. At a different level
3. With different responsibilities
4. In a whole new set of economic and other circumstances.
5. *These differences are significant and they matter significantly!*

If you are asked about salary, you need to deflect the question. Salary is talking about *you*, but you need to be talking about the *company and job*. You can deflect it in several ways. You can indicate that:

1. "While the topic of salary is important, you want to discuss it [that is, the salary for the potential job not your previous salary] once you and the employer have established a mutual interest."
2. "At the moment you are more interested in seeing if you are the right person for the job."
3. "When you two mutually decide you are the right person for the job, you are sure you and they can come to some agreement on job salary and other compensation."

Negotiation means you have to bargain for what you want. You have to do this even though many people are uncomfortable doing it. Since what you okay is what you're going to be living with for some time, you do not want to sell yourself short before you sign your contract because you will later regret it. And you definitely do NOT want to simply accept whatever you're offered *if* it doesn't match your desires without *trying* to make it closer to those desires.

WHAT ABOUT RELOCATION

Another thing you need to consider is if you'll have to relocate for this job. While you need to know as closely as possible what each compensation item is worth, evaluating your total compensation is very difficult *if* you have to move. This means you would need to find out what relocating would mean in terms of moving, housing, and the general living expenditures of the new area.

If you would have to move from Boston to Montgomery, Alabama, your overall cost of living would be lower. But if you would have to move from Montgomery to Boston, your living expenses would be considerably higher. And, of course, there are other costs associated with relocation.

With respect to the actual moving, will the employer pay the moving costs? And what about the real estate commission for selling your current house and the expenses involved in finding a new home? These are tricky particulars you will need to pin down if they want you to relocate.

Everything to which you and the employer agree needs to be in writing and part of your employment contract. You will need to receive a copy of their letter of intent which details the elements of your agreement.

WHEN THE DEAL IS FINALLY DONE

The deal "appears" to be done when the two of you agree.

Each of you has gotten something he or she desired. Ostensibly, both of you are coming away satisfied. With a handshake comes the contract or, more likely, the letter of employment.

Some companies send these documents to you. Whenever it is that you receive these documents, be sure you read the documents *very carefully* and check to see that all the items you agreed upon verbally in the employer's office are in the contract. If something is missing or misstated, you need to bring the inaccuracy to the employer's attention immediately. Only when all corrections and amendments have been made to your satisfaction should you sign the contract. The deal is truly done *only* when you sign the accurate, finalized contract.

If the contract is incorrect or lacking and the employer does not want to change it, you have to make a decision about whether to sign it or not. This will not be an easy decision to make because of all the time, effort, blood, sweat, and tears you have put into this campaign.

But always give the possibility of change a second chance. That is, you need to make sure the employer knows how you feel about this situation. You can indicate that "you want the written agreement to match the verbal agreement or you may consider going elsewhere."

When addressing this sort of situation, you need to remain calm, collected, respectful, and assertive. Anger, judgments, and accusations will only get in the way of their possibly correcting the situation. It may have been an unintentional error. Circumstances may have suddenly changed. No matter the reason, you need to be seen as handling this stressful situation in a confident problem-solving, professional way.

How you present this can make a difference. If you are going to address any such conflict, you have to present yourself as firm so the employer knows that you are serious. If you sound "squishy" or "wimpy" about this, the employer likely will not take you seriously. However, if after your discussion the employer still won't budge, your options are two: Say "good-bye" OR Take the offer.

Let me share with you the job-offer contract problem a colleague of mine encountered. A senior insurance executive with many decades of experience and a long list of accolades for her work was offered an excellent job on the East Coast which she accepted, with all negotiated items in writing. She sold her house in Indiana, moved her family to North Carolina, and bought a new house in Raleigh. But when she arrived, the recessive economy had reared its ugly head. Despite her contract, the job disappeared. So did reimbursement for her moving expenses.

The executive looked around and after more than six months finally found another executive insurance position with an emerging company. Things went smashingly through several interviews. The employer really wanted her because she had skills, expertise, and experience they sorely lacked and desperately wanted. Consequently, they verbally agreed upon an equitable salary and compensation package, comparable to what she had had previously. Everything was settled. Everything was great again.

That is, until the contract arrived by mail at her new home. On it her "agreed-upon" salary was reduced by 15 per cent. She was torn about what to do because of the relocation expenses she had already incurred and having been without a job for so long. She spoke with them but they stuck with their changed salary offer.

Despite her feelings of mistrust toward the insurance company management and her concern about their ethical principles, she finally decided to take the position at the reduced salary. This was because it gave her a salary. It was a place holder and bridge from which to look elsewhere, if she chose. Besides she knew they would offer her bonuses, which they did, in order to keep her. In the meantime she continued to network with influential others around the country, just in case the recession eased and she chose to leave for a more desirable company situation.

STILL PROMOTING ON THE JOB

Now that you're employed and part of the organization, you want to continue to present the image that helped get you the job. You created, projected, and marketed yourself as "competent-plus." So you will need to focus on continuing to dazzle them.

You will be, in effect, on probation for at least six months, with your behaviors, attitudes, and performance being carefully monitored. This means you need to go out of your way to present yourself as positive, enthusiastic, determined, motivated, and productive. In other words, just because you've gotten the job does not mean you should put all your personal presentation and promotion strategies behind you.

Likewise, you need to continue to market yourself to gain visibility and credibility inside and outside the company. You promoted yourself as a star so you don't want to just blend in and become an invisible cog in the corporate machine. Instead, you want to be seen as a team player and a committed company promoter. You can do this by:

1. Speaking at company and outside meetings
2. Writing articles for their business newsletter or for outside publications, such as relevant trade journals, trade papers, and/or the local newspapers
3. Being involved in the company's extra-curricular activities.

This will stand you in good stead for recognition in preparation for raises, bonuses, and promotions in your current job, getting a future job with another company, or going out on your own as a consultant or entrepreneur. You need to keep looking ahead because you never know if this job will disappear. Or if you simply will want to make a change to do something more advanced, less time-demanding, with more or less responsibility, or you want to new or different challenges.

Furthermore, you need to continue to network and cultivate contacts as well as find and use mentors. These individuals can help keep your skills and information up-to-date as well as alert you to other opportunities. They can also provide you with ongoing personal consultation, a sounding board for ideas, feedback, career and personal development, and problem-solving assistance.

Keep in mind: Your goals have not stopped being important just because you have gotten the job you wanted. Therefore, you need to keep your goals updated.

Specifically, you need to assess what you want to accomplish within the next five (5) years. Then, what you want to accomplish within the next ten (10) years.

Mapping out these long-range goals uses the same process you used to map out your short-range job-getting goals. This mapping will also help you determine where additional training and acquisition of new skills will be necessary and useful.

WHAT YOU'VE ACHEVED IN THIS PROCESS

Now, you need to take a moment to consider some of the many things you have achieved as a result of this job-getting process:

. You had the confidence that you could do whatever was necessary to get what you wanted.
. You realized and accepted that you chose and controlled what you did.
. You didn't allow yourself to be tossed around at everyone's whim like a ragdoll in a tornado.
. You determined how you would respond to the environment and events as they occurred.
. You decided to act to make things happen the way you wanted.
. You carefully organized your job campaign.
. You set goals, took risks, and managed your time and behavior wisely.
. You presented yourself with confidence.
. You communicated your needs and wants to others.
. You answered and asked questions.
. You persuasively "sold" yourself to the employer.
. You confidently played the interview game.

. You won the negotiation game.

. You engineered your success!

THIS IS JUST THE *BEGINNING*
NOW you need to:

1. Glow in this success and keep reminding yourself of what you *can* do to achieve your goals.

2. Keep your personal promotion strategies in place and ready for action.

3. Know what to expect the next time and prepare for it.

4. Create a generalized step-by-step plan of action for whatever large or small goal you want to achieve next.

5. Be prepared to do your assessments, research, and presentations.

6. Constantly remind yourself that you *can* now confidently and assertively handle any task, job, or career contingency.

7. Know that you *can* create success and greater job and personal satisfaction as a result whenever you want.

8. Accept that you've done it once so you can do it again ... and feel good about it.

9. Know that *only* you can set the limit on what you can achieve.

ABOUT THE AUTHOR

Signe A. Dayhoff, Ph.D., is a social psychologist who received her doctorate from Boston University where she explored how to engineer success through networking, having mentors, interpersonal communication, and social effectiveness. She handled publicity for the American Cancer Society and personal marketing consulting for solo business people and service providers.

While teaching Social Psychology and Organizational Behavior & Development at University of Massachusetts, Boston University, and Framingham State College, she produced and hosted Continental Cablevision's career-development/personal marketing (presentation and promotion) program, the *Inside Track*, in Wellesley, Massachusetts, for four years. For it she received the Continental Cablevision's Conti Award nomination.

She is the author of 15 other books including:

. *Create Your Own Career Opportunities*, a guide to self-promotion through creating visibility and credibility
. *Diagonally-Parked in a Parallel Universe: Working Through Social Anxiety* (2nd Edition)
. *Promote Myself? I'd Rather Eat Worms!*
. *Scared of Your Boss? Smash Through Your Fear Now Course*
. *How to Speak Without Fear Small Talk Course*
. *Get The Job You Want*
. *Decision Making For Managers* (for AMACOM's Education for Management).
. Contributed to books such as Steven J. Bennett's

Executive Chess: Creative Problem Solving by 45 of America's Top Business Leaders and Thinkers.

Founding The Mentoring Network, she showed individuals how to communicate, present and promote themselves more confidently, network, and use mentors to effectively achieve their goals. She created a mentoring program for the headquarters of the American Red Cross and has presented her research findings nationally and on radio and television.

She has been quoted in publications including *Industry Week*, *Wall Street Journal*, *Boston Business Journal*, *Success*, *Executive Travel*, *Time Out New York*, *Shape*, and *Cosmopolitan*.

In her spare time she is an applied feline behaviorist and "kitty mom" to 20-plus rescued elderly, disabled, and special-needs cats. As a result, she has authored cat memoirs including:

. *What Faust the Dancing Cat Taught Me*
. *Remarkable Tales of Cats Who Whisper to Humans*
. *How Intrepid the Disabled Kitten Triumphed to Help Others.*